INTELLECTUALS AND THE LEFT IN FRANCE
SINCE 1968

By the same author

THE CINEMA: A HISTORY
CULTURES ON CELLULOID

INTELLECTUALS AND THE LEFT IN FRANCE SINCE 1968

Keith A. Reader

Senior Lecturer in French
Kingston Polytechnic

St. Martin's Press   New York

© Keith A. Reader 1987

All rights reserved. For information, write:
Scholarly & Reference Division,
St. Martin's Press, Inc., 175 Fifth Avenue, New York, NY 10010

First published in the United States of America in 1987

Printed in Hong Kong

ISBN 0-312-41894-9

Library of Congress Cataloging in Publication Data
Reader, Keith.
Intellectuals and the Left in France since 1968.
1. France—Intellectual life—20th century.
2. France—Politics and government—1958–
3. Intellectuals—France—Political activity.
4. Politics and culture—France.
5. Right and left (Political science).
I. Title
DC415.R43   1987   944.092   85–22159
ISBN 0-312-41894-9

For E. K. with love

Contents

Acknowledgements

I should like to thank in particular:
Paul Bensimon, Philippe Binet, Jean-Louis Fabiani, Jill Forbes, Michael
Hawkins, Eleonore Kofman, Colin MacCabe, Richard Nice, Catherine
Schmidt, and Hervé Touboul, for ideas, suggestions, and discussion; the
members of the Modern Critical Theory Group, for provoking thought
about Chapter 6 in particular; the Nuffield Foundation, for a grant
which enabled me to spend part of the summer of 1983 in Paris
researching this book; the staff of the Bibliothèque de la Maison des
Sciences de l'Homme and of the Bibliothèque du Centre Georges
Pompidou (Beaubourg) in Paris, and Madeleine Evans and Claire
Hutton of Kingston Polytechnic Library, for their help and kindness; my
colleagues in the Faculty of Arts and Languages at Kingston Polytechnic, in particular Chris Cobb and all the members of the French
section, for enabling me to take a term's study-leave without which the
book would never have been completed; Chris Cook, for advice on the
world of publishing; and, above all, my parents and Eleonore, for their
warm and loving support.

Preface

A great deal has happened during the past seventeen years to draw attention within the English-speaking world to the relationship between intellectuals and the Left in France. The 'events' of 1968, while in many ways anti-intellectual, were inseparable from the universities, where they started and where their most lasting effects were felt. Thirteen years later, the election of a Socialist President – who was also something of an intellectual – was seen variously as the logical consequence or the diluted aftermath of the cultural upheaval of May. Intellectual discussion of the 'two Mays', not only in universities or learned journals, but in the national press and on radio or television, achieved a prominence almost impossible to imagine in the society of Britain or the United States.

Intellectuals have always occupied a place at once more influential and more critical of the established social order – hence, loosely, more 'left-wing' – in French than in British or American society. Part of the *raison d'être* of this book is to look at why this should be so and how it has manifested itself between 1968 and the present day. The tendency has been for the English-speaking world to encounter major recent developments in French intellectual life by way of a series of 'names' (Althusser, Deleuze, Derrida, Foucault, Kristeva, Lacan) which recur inescapably in any discussion of the period. This, while inevitable given the pervasiveness of the French intellectual 'star-system', is also profoundly ironic, for all the writers mentioned (and not only they) have significantly undermined the notions of individuality and personal autonomy on which Western philosophical and political discourse has been based since its inception. The paradox that Lacan, who gave the first full and radical account of the intimate connections between language and patriarchy, should at the same time have set himself up as the Great Linguistic Patriarch *par excellence*, or that Derrida, whose deconstructive analyses call the very existence of a pre-given text into question, should regularly figure as a 'set author' on American literary and philosophical syllabuses – these have been often remarked upon, and are not irrelevant to this study. Beyond the scope they afford for ironic amusement, they have important political and institutional implications, reflecting the perception of the French intellectual as a uniquely prolific and privileged species. The Frankfurt School in Germany, the Bloomsbury Group in Britain, Gramsci in Italy are all examples of intellectuals inseparably linked with the social formations from which they arose, but the sheer number and range of 'Latin Quarter' intellectuals sets them apart from any other group, and in so doing may actually divert attention from the importance of the various contexts – political, social, and institutional – within which they worked. 'Althusser', 'Derrida', 'Lacan', often seem to exist in no context other than that bounded, in scholarly journals or tables of reference, by their own names and the litany of which they form part. What will not be found here, then, is yet another summary of the key ideas of 'pantheon' thinkers. Ample work of this kind (some of it excellent, some indifferent or worse) has already been carried out, and it would have been superfluous to add to it. Emphasis falls rather on the specifically French contexts of their work, so that while there is no dearth of intellectual 'names' the focus will also be on the different institutions, from the University of Paris – VIII (Vincennes) to the French Communist Party or the television programme *Apostrophes*, which have influenced the work here discussed. My hope is that even readers already familiar with many of the ideas and writers dealt with here will find a kind of contextualisation not otherwise readily available in English.

There are, on the other hand, a great many thinkers whose work still awaits adequate treatment in English, at least in book form. I cannot claim, in so limited a compass, to have achieved that here; but I hope that what I say about the work of figures as important as Lyotard or Bourdieu may provide a helpful contextualising introduction.

Finally, I should make some attempt to explain my choice of writers and texts. For the former, the division just mentioned gives the rationale: certain figures cried out for some form of introduction and treatment, others – the better-known and more extensively written-about – are frequently dealt with out of their French context and benefit from an understanding of that dimension. Those I have omitted have been, inevitably, on grounds of space (with the craven value-judgement that implies), or a feeling of inadequacy in their particular field (which, and not a judgement of value, accounts for, for example, the absence of economists).

For text-choice, the criteria were more complex. Obvious key works in an author's output – Bourdieu's *La Distinction*, Luce Irigaray's *Ce sexe qui n'en est pas un* – selected themselves if their authors were still (relatively) little-known to an anglophone public. With certain notably prolific figures, such as Henri Lefebvre, there was an inevitable choice between superficiality in the treatment of a large number of works and arbitrariness in the exclusion of many. Given the importance of close contextualisation, I opted for the second alternative, choosing for analysis works representing key periods at once in their author's output and in the development of French society.

With the 'superstars', however, my criteria for choice were different again. Apparently minor or 'occasional' writings may achieve a seemingly unjustified prominence here, but this is so only if one is considering them *sub specie aeternitatis*, which I am certainly not. The contemporary significance of Sartre's or Derrida's work is better brought out, at least in a political context, by an examination of *Situations* or *Positions* than by adding to the weight of existing material on *L'Idiot de la Famille* or *Marges de la philosophie*, more conceptually substantial though these may be.

For all the above, there will inevitably be omissions, injustices, and inaccuracies in these pages, and I should like to take this opportunity of apologising to all offended by them.

A few notes, finally, about style and linguistic problems. I have referred to each work mentioned in French, with an English translation of the title on its first appearance only (except with obvious examples such as *Situations*). Quotations are in English throughout – sometimes my own translation from the French, sometimes taken directly from a published translation. Footnote acknowledgement is always given in the latter case. The words 'modern' and 'contemporary', often treated as synonymous in English, I have found helpful to use in their distinctive French senses: 'modern' referring to a broader time-span and 'contemporary' to the immediate past (here generally since 1968).

A short list of frequently-used initials is provided; the book should thus be readable by those with no knowledge whatever of French.

K.A.R.

List of Abbreviations

PCF   Parti Communiste Français – the French Communist Party

JCR   Jeunesse Communiste Révolutionnaire – leading Trotskyist group in May 1968; now known as the Ligue Communiste Révolutionnaire (LCR)

PSU   Parti Socialiste Unifié – a workers'-control centred, non-Leninist Leftist grouping that came to the fore in May 1968

FHAR   Front Homosexuel d'Action Révolutionnaire – Revolutionary Homosexual Front; a far-left, gay group of the early 1970s

GREPH   Groupe de Recherche sur l'Enseignement Philosophie – founded by Derrida in response to threats to lessen the importance of philosophy in the educational curriculum

CAPES   Certificat d'Aptitude au Professorat de l'Enseignement du Second Degré – a competitive examination to recruit secondary-school teachers

1 The May 'Events' – What Were They?

In May 1968, a student protest against restricted visiting-rights in university hostels sparked off a movement which brought virtually the whole of France to a halt, yet culminated anti-climactically in an increased Gaullist majority in the July general election. What happened was variously described as an aborted social revolution of a qualitatively new kind, a gesture of youthful revolt against a tired and patronising society, a symptom of all that was wrong with established French politics alike of the Right and of the Left, a toytown pseudo-revolution staged by an insignificant group of spoiled and idle rich, and the greatest strike in history. The fact that the last two judgements came from members of the Parti Communiste Français, the PCF, (the former is a not unfair condensation of the statements made by its General Secretary, Georges Marchais, at the time; the latter the verdict of Louis Althusser, then the Party's leading intellectual, nine years afterwards) is sufficient indication of how difficult it was, and remains, to assess exactly what happened in 1968. This is figured in the very manner in which it is generally referred to – either simply as 'May' or as 'les événements' ('the events') – anodine lowest common denominators for a date, and a series of movements, that were immediately recognised as some kind of watershed in French history.

On 10 May 1981, at the second ballot and contrary to most expectations, François Mitterrand, the Socialist candidate, became President of France. It was the first time for thirty-four years that the country had been governed by the Left, and after the disappointments first of July 1968, then of March 1978 when the 'Common Programme' of Socialists, Communists, and Left Radicals had fallen disastrously apart before the parliamentary elections, the news was greeted ecstatically. The Place de la Bastille (symbol of the 1789 Revolution) and the Place de la République (traditional rallying-point for French working-class movements and demonstrations) were filled with cheering, carousing crowds; many factories were forced to close as their workers

1

flocked to celebrate; the festive atmosphere of May 1968 seemed to have returned, this time with political power on its side.

In January 1982, the newspaper *Le Quotidien de Paris* began the publication of a series of short articles from intellectuals commenting (often in highly critical vein) on the Mitterrand regime. In the following year, these texts were published under the title *Socrate et la Rose* [*Socrates and the Rose*] (the first term referring to the traditional social-critical role of the intellectual, the second to the emblem of the Socialist Party). In August 1983, when the Socialist Government's unpopularity was marked and increasing, *Le Monde* published a letter from Max Gallo, writer and Socialist minister, deploring 'the silence of the left-wing intellectuals'. This inaugurated a lengthy correspondence which had its niche on the newspaper's front page for most of the traditionally sacrosanct vacation month and even provoked an irritated comment from one reader who had found it still going on when he returned from holiday.

What these apparently unrelated episodes – a major cultural upheaval, a major political change, and a brief flurry of articles and letters – have in common is that they spotlight in different ways the relationship between the intellectual and the political sphere that has long been characteristic of French society. May 1968 meant among other things a refusal of traditional forms of intellectual and political life, most notably in the traditional meeting-place of the two, the university. Mitterrand's candidacy was supported by a great many prominent French intellectuals (Simone de Beauvoir even broke a lifetime's habit of abstention by voting for him), and the number of teachers in the Assembly and the Government led to comparisons with the *république des professeurs* of the late 1920s.

To try to conceive of a British newspaper or magazine devoting a column for nearly a month to the silence of left-wing intellectuals beggars the imagination, and in so doing provides an eloquent comment on the very different relations between intellectual and political life that exist in France.

We therefore need to begin by looking at the reasons, historical and structural, for the consistently greater prominence of intellectuals in French society. Two key events here are the French Revolution and the Dreyfus Affair – the first dramatically overthrowing the landed aristocracy and instituting the first bourgeois nation-state, the second dividing the whole of French society along political lines and mobilising many of the nation's leading intellectuals behind Dreyfus. Without the work of Rousseau and the *idéologues*, the very concepts of liberty, equality, and fraternity would have been difficult to imagine, so that it is possible to speak of 1789 as in a very real sense an intellectual phenomenon. Gramsci, in his essay *The Formation of Intellectuals*, emphasises how, while every social class 'creates with itself, organically, one or more groups of intellectuals',[1] the capitalist class requires a much more rapid and sophisticated proliferation than its predecessors, representing as it does a much more complex and intensive development of social resources.

For both these reasons, then, it is not surprising that the French Revolution and the social change it engendered placed the intelligentsia in the forefront of French society. This tendency was further encouraged by two major phenomena of the period: the centralisation of power and authority upon Paris and the educational meritocracy of *grandes écoles*. Both had as their object the eradication of the corruption that had been so widespread among the aristocracy; both are still so entrenched as now almost to be considered structural rather than historical, but for that very reason are worth resituating in the context of their origin – that of the first modern European nation-state and the importance it attached to the formation of (to borrow a term from Gramsci) its 'organic intellectuals'.

That the *parti pris* of the French intelligentsia has traditionally been of the Left becomes easier to understand in this light. This allegiance has, of course, been transformed and called into question since 1968, but it is worth making the point at the outset that the 'special relationship' inaugurated by the Jacobin and Napoleonic regimes is still in existence. The PCF claimed in an interview early in 1981 that its membership included 70 000 intellectuals – a definition elastic enough to include journalists, engineering and technical executives, 'artists' of various kinds, and generally those whom the British Labour Party would define as workers 'by brain' rather than 'by hand'. Virtually all the leading names in what Régis Debray calls the 'upper intelligentsia' have at some time claimed some degree of allegiance to the Left, though this may have been little more than an acknowledgement of the conceptual utility of the Marxist dialectic (as with Lévi-Strauss). Conversely, an attempt to convene a forum of right-wing intellectuals in December 1981, under the title 'Alternatives to Socialism', was a resounding fiasco; and even the 'new philosophers' acquired much of their notoriety through their spectacular public recantations of their previous enthusiasm for the far Left.

It was the Dreyfus affair, and in particular the 'intellectuals' manifesto', that appeared in *L'Aurore* in 1898, that first demonstrated the impact intellectuals could have upon the processes of practical politics. The manifesto, instigated by Zola, was signed by an impressive range of names including Anatole France, Marcel Proust (something of a 'salon pink' in his socially active days), Lucien Herr (librarian at the École Normale Supérieure, and a leading proponent of socialist ideas), and one of Herr's 'disciples' – Léon Blum, later to become head of the Popular Front government. The right-wing writer Maurice Barrès stigmatised the signatories as a 'bunch of semi-intellectuals', who did not 'feel spontaneously at one with their natural group' – a judgement in tune with Barrès's provincial loathing for the cosmopolitan world of the Parisian intelligentsia. Interestingly, the word 'intellectuel' had first been used as a noun in French only twelve years earlier, so that for Barrès's audience it would still have been something of a neologism. Barrès's use certainly helped to give the term the pejorative force it undoubtedly had in its early days; however, history took its revenge on semantics with the rehabilitation of Dreyfus and the consequent vindication of his defenders. This would not have happened without Zola's efforts on Dreyfus's behalf and his success in mobilising so much of the intelligentsia, and the notion that intellectuals as a body could in certain situations exert specific forms of political power rapidly became accepted. In the years after the Second World War, manifestos and petitions signed by intellectuals (invariably including Sartre) became commonplace in French society; René Lourau goes so far as to describe them, in *Le Lapsus des Intellectuels* [*The Intellectuals' Slip*], as 'pure effects of the intelligentsia's star-system'[2]. It seems clear that much of the mystique of the intellectual petition can be traced back to the 'manifesto' and the Dreyfus Affair.

Socialist though many of the Dreyfus signatories and other prominent intellectuals of the time were, there was no sense in which any of them could have been described as Marxist. The foundation of the PCF after the Tours split of 1920, and the interest aroused by the Russian Revolution, helped to place Marxism ('scientific socialism') upon the political and intellectual agenda. A wave of Russophilia swept through the French intelligentsia, similar to the Sinophilia that was an important factor in and after 1968, and writers such as Gide, Barbusse, and Aragon (who remained faithful for the rest of his life) either joined the PCF or publicly expressed sympathy with it. It is hardly surprising that intellectuals, whose avocation as a species is the systematic pursuit of truth, should have been attracted by the pursuit of systematic truth that is Marxism, nor that the guiltily ineffectual feelings by which intellectuals of the Left are traditionally assailed should have caused many of them to turn to that hard-nosed fusion of theory and practice they hoped to find in the PCF.

What conferred upon Marxism and the PCF particular strength and credibility, however, was the Second World War and the Resistance. The leading role played by the PCF at home and the USSR abroad; the pertinence of Marxist analyses of Fascism and Nazism, their refusal to rely on flatulent rhetoric about 'humanity's bottomless capacity for evil' and like choice phrases; the educative role played by cadres with their companions in the army (well illustrated by Brunet in Sartre's *Les Chemins de la Liberté*) – all went to increase the persuasiveness of the Marxist alternative to old-school humanistic socialism. Althusser himself was recruited to the Party through his experiences in a concentration camp.

The milieu with which Sartre especially was associated after the war – Saint-Germain-des-Prés, home of jazz-cellars, late-night cafés, and a passion for American culture among those who most vociferously denounced American politics – was in many respects the polar opposite of the PCF. Saint-Germain was wilfully independent, resolutely unstructured, and uncommitted to any programme other than that of radical self-inquiry. To describe it as an 'intellectual' milieu is only partially true; it resembled rather a revival of the nineteenth-century *vie de Bohème*, where the 'intellectual' and the 'artistic' flowed into each other around the same café tables. Many of its denizens would probably have recoiled in distaste from any suggestion of direct political involvement, yet the milieu is important from our point of view because it opened the possibility of a way of life outside the strait-jacket of the French bourgeois family. Much of Saint-Germain's reputation for sexual and behavioural permissiveness now appears comically passé, but it provided (as a reading of *Les Chemins de la Liberté* or Simone de Beauvoir's *Les Mandarins* will show) a model for escaping the tyranny which the French family, through its structures and tradition, could not help imposing on its members.

It was also a stimulating milieu that encouraged individuality, not the first words that spring to mind when one thinks of the post-war PCF. The sorry state of Communist intellectual life under the Stalinist yoke is sufficiently well known not to need detailed exposition here, but it is important to bear in mind that many of the developments that led up to and followed from 1968 were directly related to it. The work of such Party intellectuals as Garaudy, Althusser, and Balibar was seen as particularly important because of the low ebb of intellectual life in the

Party during the forties and fifties, and much of the Party's unpopularity among those active in 'the events' can be traced back to the systematic repression of cultural and conceptual individuality that characterised it in the 'Stalin years'.

As mentioned in the Preface to this book, May 1968 – where our story really starts – was not (or not strictly, or not primarily) an intellectual movement. The word that best distils the spirit of the time is 'imagination', present in or behind the wall-slogans that were such an important feature of May: 'Power to the imagination'; 'Take your desires for reality'; 'Beneath the paving-stones, the beach'. These, along with more overtly political (?) graffiti such as 'I'm a Marxist – of the Groucho faction', are reminiscent of the heyday of Surrealism rather than of any more overtly political influence. To be sure, political movements of the Left were active throughout May. The Jeunesse Communiste Révolutionnaire provided most of the stewards for the major demonstrations; a great many of the Catholics who took part in or supported the movement subsequently became active in non-Leninist groupings such as the Partie Socialiste Unifié (PSU); and, as we shall see in more detail shortly, the names of Che Guevara and Mao Zedong were everywhere. This had much to do with the way in which the PCF had totally lost touch with youth, and with its quintessentially unimaginative attitude towards a movement fuelled by imagination – with, in other words, the chasm between a politics focused on the industrial working class and a sudden eruption of the imaginative qualities that the French family, educational, and political systems had consistently denied. Not until the Socialist victory of 1981 was it even possible for anybody to say that that gulf was being bridged, and subsequent events have cast doubt even on that.

The overtly political legacy of May, in other words, was a long-term phenomenon, and much of the difficulty of assessing what the 'events' actually *were* stems from their bewildering juxtaposition of the ephemeral and the lasting. The landscape of West European politics would not be what it is today without them; the importance of sexual politics, environmental and ecological issues, workers' control and co-operative movements, and the politics of culture for the European Left became qualitatively different after May. Yet the legislative elections held as a result of the 'events' produced a landslide Gaullist majority. The narrowly political significance of May is not part of our brief here, but it seems that it is in many ways analogous to its intellectual significance. May represented an insurrection against outdated and repressive structures, political, social, cultural, and intellectual; and, because that insurrection was so unexpected and in many ways so unco-ordinated, its results were felt unpredictably, in widely different times and ways across different areas. The dominant intellectual mode before May had been that known as 'structuralist' – a term more and more frequently used with less and less precision. Most of the work to which the term can properly be applied was carried out before 1968, initially piecemeal but rapidly becoming a sustained critique of the founding notions of bourgeois humanism. Ferdinand de Saussure, in his *Cours de Linguistique Générale* [*Course in General Linguistics*] (published as early as 1916), emphasised the manner in which language functions as a system of differences, moving away from the historical view of language as an entity unfolding organically towards an analysis of how meaning is produced – independently of individual human agency – by the articulation of signifier and signified. Claude Lévi-Strauss's *Anthropologie Structurale* [*Structural Anthropology*] analysed myth as a society's means of resolving conflicts and dilemmas it could not openly admit to; again, the stress was on how patterns of similarity and difference, rather than demiurgic, individual entities, produce meaning. Althusser, in *Pour Marx* [*For Marx*] and *Lire le Capital* [*Reading Capital*], produced rigorous rereadings of Marx's major texts which emphasised the anti-humanism of Marxist thought and the complex structuring of the dialectic.

But it was Michel Foucault's *Les Mots et les Choses* [*The Order of Things*], published in 1966, that attracted more widespread attention than any other 'structuralist' work, despite Foucault's rejection of the label. *Les Mots et les Choses* is a complex work of epistemological history, subtitled 'an archaeology of the human sciences', and tracing the evolution from a society predicated on discourse to one predicated on Man, which was now in its turn being supplanted by the 'return' of language. The development of anthropology, psychoanalysis, and modern literature were all seen by Foucault as calling the notion of a unified human nature into question. What made the book a major phenomenon outside the academic world – almost a *succès de scandale* – was its often-quoted assertion that 'if we study thought as an archaeologist studies buried cities, we can see that Man was born yesterday, and that he soon may die'. As John Ardagh says in the passage on *France in the 1980s* in which he quotes and discusses this: 'An educated public reacted with fascinated horror at a new philosophy which made even Sartre's ideas look humane and optimistic. Sartre had killed God; the structuralists were killing Man too!'[3]

This view of Foucault's work, and that of the other 'structuralists', was in fact based on a misapprehension, which has profoundly affected the perception of them in the English-speaking world in particular. The stress placed by all these writers on the importance of structures that go beyond individual free will, and the manner in which all their work makes it clear that the nineteenth-century, bourgeois–humanist definition of 'Man' has outlived itself, emphatically does not mean that the individual agent is merely 'the prisoner of a determined system' (to quote John Ardagh, reproducing the fallacy under discussion). The removal of the illusion of human autonomy does not consign all purposive human activity to the domain of the utopian. If it did, Althusser would presumably never have joined the PCF, nor Foucault (certainly on the basis of Russell's paradox about sets which are not members of themselves) been able to extract himself from the resultant aporia and write *Les Mots et les Choses*. Psychoanalysis and anthropology, even as they undid the illusions on which the Western sociopolitical order had been based, thereby made the task of intervening in that order paradoxically easier, for its epistemological Achilles' heel had been laid bare.

This in turn means that those who saw the May events as a triumphant spontaneist refutation of structuralist gloom had radically misinterpreted what the 'structuralist' thinkers were about. It would have been more convincing to have considered the Gaullist victory in July as a gloomy structuralist refutation of triumphalist spontaneism. The breaking-down of traditional disciplinary barriers by the thinkers mentioned formed part of the same rejection of an outmoded academic world as the student revolt. The cultural and the political, in May, were no longer apparently distinct spheres; the literary and cultural criticism of Roland Barthes and Pierre Macherey, the importance of literature in the work of Foucault and Lacan, or of psychoanalysis in that of Althusser, provided extensive theoretical vindication of that perception. To see the May events, however unstructured they may have been, as the antithesis of structuralism is too simple a view by half. It is nevertheless true that the dominant intellectual influence during May was not that of the Left Bank 'structuralists'. It came rather from outside Europe – from California, where the émigré German Herbert Marcuse was a professor of philosophy, from South America and the revolutionary example of Che Guevara, and from the China of Mao Zedong. Marcuse's *One-Dimensional Man* was a key text of what might be called the 'socialism of affluence', all but writing-off the industrial working class as 'recuperated' by the blandishments of the consumer society and seeking the mainsprings of revolution instead in those outside the productive process, above all students. Nowadays it reads like a bizarrely optimistic amalgam of 1950s 'affluent worker' sociology, gently politicised hippiedom, and Lenin's *What is to be Done?*; but, while its revolutionary predictions were somewhat over-sanguine, it was important because of the possibilities it indicated for groups outside the traditional Communist constituency of blue-collar workers.

Che Guevara was an icon rather than an ideological catalyst – the poster on countless walls reminding intellectuals that one of their number had made the supreme sacrifice in the cause of social justice, and that another (Régis Debray, an important figure in our study) was paying in a Bolivian prison the price for his commitment to that same justice in the Third World. Anger and guilt at the French colonial record in North Africa (above all in Algeria) had been an important factor in radicalising many French people in the 1950s and early 1960s, politicising a good many Catholics in particular, rather as developments in Latin America are doing now. This was compounded at the time of May by disillusionment with the 'workerist' approach of the PCF, which predisposed many younger people to look outside France, or even Europe, for a model of what a less hidebound form of socialism might be like. Castro's Cuba and the rest of Latin America in struggle provided one beacon; more important still – in fact perhaps the single most important figure of May, in its very ambiguity – was Mao Zedong.

'Figure' ought really to read 'figures', for there were two 'Mao Zedongs' in the France of 1968, and the confusion between them was an important factor in developments thereafter. Mao Zedong as political ruler of China and Marxist theoretician was the arch 'anti-revisionist', by which is meant that he condemned the de-Stalinisation that followed Khruschev's speech to the Twentieth Congress of the Soviet Communist Party in 1956. For Mao and his more dogmatic acolytes, Stalin was the true heir of the Leninist tradition of disciplined party organisation, materialist purism, and the subordination of bourgeois–humanist notions of freedom, democracy, and justice to the overriding demands of the class-struggle and the building of Communism – all of which is exemplified in one of Mao's most celebrated dicta, 'Put politics in command'. It was this 'version' of Mao that came into an embarrassing kind of prominence for many of his former disciples, in France and elsewhere, when the full horrors of the Cultural Revolution came to light after his death.

The 'other Mao' – the poster guru of 1968 – was a more appealing figure, but also a less politically coherent and incisive one. What gave this myth its resonance was, on the one hand, widespread disillusionment with the USSR and the attention focused on the Far East by the Vietnam War (originally a French colonial conflict); on the other, equally widespread enthusiasm for a hideously sanitised version of the Cultural Revolution. The idea that the cultural and intellectual spheres could become major areas of political struggle had an obvious appeal for intellectuals of the Left, and the view of Chinese society as a hive of cultural democracy, buzzing with wall-newspapers and street theatre, was given credence by Mao's own activity as a poet and carefully cultivated image as the Third World's first Renaissance Man. It all seemed very different from the iron fist of socialist realism in the USSR. This second image of Mao is now all too easy to mock, but what is important here is its diagnostic value. It pointed, especially when taken in conjunction with elements of the 'first Mao', to what left-wing intellectuals during and after May were seeking: a kind of politics that on the one hand enlarged the scope for cultural and intellectual action, and on the other made it possible to offset guilty liberal woolliness with a vigorous transfusion of Marxist–Leninist 'science'.

The best example of this is provided by the summer 1968 issue of the magazine *Tel Quel.* This, edited by the novelist and literary theoretician Philippe Sollers, was for many years the leading French avant-garde literary journal; it changed its publisher and its name (to *L'Infini*) in 1982. May 1968 was described in the summer issue as 'the Revolution, here and now', and the Parisian 'Cultural Revolution' was given an ambitious programme signed among others by the cinematic theoretician Jean-Louis Baudry, the composer and conductor Pierre Boulez, the literary theoreticians Julia Kristeva and Jean Ricardou, and Sollers himself (Kristeva's husband).

The programme was to be amplified and discussed by a 'Group for Theoretical Studies', which was to meet weekly. Extensive quotation is necessary to convey the flavour of this rigorous yet all-embracing enterprise and how it figured the transcending of disciplinary barriers that was such an important part of the contemporary French landscape, here placed under the scientific banner of Marxism-Leninism:

5: The construction of a theory drawn from the kind of textual practice we have to develop therefore seems to us capable of avoiding the repeated blind alleys of 'committed' discourse – that model of telelogico-transcendental humanist and psychologist mystification, complicit with the definitive obscurantism of the bourgeois state.

6: This construction will have to form a part, in accordance with its complex mode of production, of Marxist-Leninist theory, the only revolutionary theory of our time, and work towards the critical integration of the most developed practices of philosophy, linguistics, semiology, psychoanalysis, 'literature', and the history of science.

7: Any ideological undertaking which does not today present itself in an advanced theoretical form and settles instead for bringing together under eclectic or sentimental headings individual and under-politicised activities, seems to us counter-revolutionary, inasmuch as it fails to recognise the process of the class-struggle, which has objectively to be carried on and reactivated.[4]

The programmatic numbering of clauses; the unequivocal labelling of theoretical (hence political) enemies; the objective identification of 'utopian' or 'sentimental' Left and reactionary Right; the priority unequivocally given to the waging of the class-struggle – these are traits that the *Tel Quel* text had in common with other 'Marxist–Leninist–Maoist' documents of the time. The second image of Mao is present in the importance attached to cultural intervention on a par with other, apparently more 'political' kinds, notably through the invitation to specialists from a host of different areas to work together in and for the grand Marxist cultural commonwealth, and also through the kinds of text singled out as politically desirable by *Tel Quel* and those associated with it.

'Committed literature' had, as the text quite correctly pointed out, run itself into one blind alley after another – so much so that Sartre himself had by this time all but abandoned literature for commitment. Socialist realism unfortunately produced texts that no self-respecting Left Bank intellectual would ever want to read. What was called for instead, in the pages of *Tel Quel* and elsewhere, was a radical subverting of the individual's secure self-identification in language: his or her *subjectivity*, understood as the manner in which individuals recognise themselves as subjects in and of any linguistic text. This is well illustrated by Althusser's account of how bourgeois ideology '"recruits" subjects among the individuals or "transforms" the individuals into subjects by that very precise operation which I have called *interpellation* or hailing, and which can be imagined along the lines of the most commonplace everyday police (or other) hailing: "Hey, you there!"'[5]

What is important here is the kind of 'textual politics' to which this conception gave rise. The linguistic and formal experiments of the *nouveau roman*, and of earlier writers such as Rabelais, Kafka, and above all Joyce – these became the focus of a political theory of literature. The sociologist Pierre Bourdieu (dealt with in detail in Chapter 10) has devoted much of his work to the elaboration and exposure of an ideology of 'distinction' (the title of his *magnum opus*), emphasising how intellectuals reinforce their 'aristocratic' position in French society by privileging often arcane and theoretically 'pure' theories and types of work. There can be few better illustrations of this than the manner in which the formal intricacies of modernist writing – much criticised by 'old-school' Marxist theoreticians such as Georg Lukàcs – were promoted to a vanguard political role, by virtue of being not outside the productive process like Marcuse's students but *inside* it, bodying forth the productive processes of language and subjectivity in the most sophisticatedly deconstructive manner.

Feminist critics were later to attack some of the writers elevated to the *Tel Quel* pantheon (the Marquis de Sade, Nietzsche, Georges Bataille) for varying types of misogyny; and the thrust of Bourdieu's exposure of the ideology of distinction is in a different way implicitly critical of the ideas associated with the journal. Thus, symptomatically, one major omission from writing in this area was any consideration of what the likely audience or readership for a text might be. The public was hypostatised in such a way as to suggest that a progressive text remained a progressive text regardless of by whom or in what context it was being read.

This was partly because the context in which this work went on was a geographically and socially confined one. French intellectual life is over-whelmingly concentrated on Paris, and within Paris on the confined area of the fifth, sixth, and seventh *arrondissements*; this means that intellec-tuals who in Britain would know one another only by reputation, or through fleeting encounters at academic conferences, are in France likely to be close neighbours in the most literal geographical sense. Such a concentration (wittily anathematised by Hervé Hamon and Patrick Rotman in *Les Intellocrates*) is bound to encourage a narrowing of perspective implicitly elitist in its results.

The intellectual world of the Left Bank is, for Hamon and Rotman, structured by historical and ideological as well as geographical affinities. The main groups they identify include, as well as ex-Communists ('the largest party in France') and Catholics radicalised by their opposition to the Algerian War, those known as *les soixante-huitards*. This umbrella term covers all those who took part in, or were affected by, the ideas and spirit of 'the events', and there is no doubt that their continuing influence on French cultural and economic life is an extremely important one. The major 'names' of May have been politically discredited (Mao), socially and economically outdated (Marcuse), or perhaps too readily dismissed as epiphenomena (Daniel Cohn-Bendit); but the 'spirit of the times' lives on, and it is to the concretisation of that somewhat idealistic expression that it is now necessary to turn.

The dethroning of economism from its place at the centre of left-wing thought is the most pervasive and abiding legacy of May. The example of the *Tel Quel* manifesto and the 'politics of subjectivity' illustrates this well. It was no longer necessary for intellectuals of the Left to turn themselves into socialist realists, try to get themselves arrested on demonstrations, or reserve their political energies for trade-union or party-political activity. The cultural and academic domains were recognised as major areas of struggle in their own right, and this was identified by the wholesale reorganisation of French universities after May. The old structures, centralised and authoritarian beyond belief, were replaced by more open forms of management, greater freedom in the drafting and launching of courses, and the possibility for different institutions to develop their own academic and ideological identity. The University of Paris–VIII (Vincennes), founded after May to develop access to higher education for part-time students and those without formal qualifications, was the best example of the attitudes that became widespread in the academic world after May. Rumours of sexual and narcotic excess at Vincennes provoked a sensationalised hostility on the Right which eventually led to the literal demolition of its buildings and the university's removal, in a much enfeebled form, to Saint-Denis. What is important here is the way in which the variety of new areas opened up after 1968 changed and broadened the terrain of politicised intellectual debate.

This in its turn affected the different analyses of May offered by writers and intellectuals, both immediately after (or even during) the events and on the occasion of their tenth anniversary. Edgar Morin, in *La commune étudiante* [*The student commune*], gave a somewhat utopian description of the events as 'perhaps a model for the coming mutations of Western society';[6] but his analysis did at least point to one of the fundamental problems posed by the movement, through its ambivalent attitude towards the relevance of educational qualifications to contemporary society. On the one hand, there was dissatisfaction with the dwindling number of opportunities for well-qualified students; on the other, disgust with the way in which the social sciences in particular had been pressed into the service of *le pouvoir* (power), a term that embraced not only the Gaullist regime but the other regimes – of knowledge, containment, social control – at work in society. (The work of Michel Foucault is the major theoretical elaboration of this.) The eclecticism of the movement – another quality singled out by Morin – sprang largely from this ambivalence; it was able to draw together everybody, from already-committed Marxist revolutionaries to hitherto unpoliticised students concerned that their studies neither guaranteed them a worthwhile job nor gave them intellectual and personal satisfaction.

The currents identified by Morin unsurprisingly include revolutionary Marxism, anarchism (long a potent ideological force in France), and various Gallic forms of 'radical chic'. 'Maoism' in the looser of its two forms drew on all these. Also important for Morin and other writers on May were two currents less easy to pin down ideologically: radical Christianity – in 1968, as during the Algerian War, an important source of ethical criticism and strength; and the movement known as 'situationism'. This tendency, later influential in the work of Jean Baudrillard (see Chapter 10), attacked above all the 'society of the spectacle' – the manner in which modern society marginalises most of its members, reducing even those seemingly most involved in the political process to the effective status of passive observers. Like much else in May, the situationists were not to survive for long as an active political force, but were to have much influence on the large-scale rethinking of what the 'political' might be that went on after 1968.

This rethinking was greatly stimulated by what the sociologist Alain Touraine, in *Le mouvement de mai ou le communisme utopique* [*The May movement or utopian communism*], calls 'the new social movements' – later to embrace ecology, feminism, anti-nuclear activity, Third World politics, and other developments that took place on the margins of hitherto established political life and in opposition to the dominant technological bureaucracy. The upsurge of the Parti Socialiste, which came into being from a number of other groupings in 1971 and within ten years was the majority party of government; the PCF's eventually unsuccessful attempt to leave behind its Stalinist image and take more account of the new groupings, or even recuperate them under the 'Eurocommunist' banner – these all owed much to the movements that came to the fore in May. There is no doubt that movements that, as with feminism or 'Eurocommunism', often sprang from an intellectual milieu and had much influence on intellectual life, played a major part in the renaissance of the Left that culminated in 1981.

Many commentators on the events were somewhat baffled by the manner in which they implicitly redefined the political. Thus, Raymond Aron, doyen of French ex-Communists, spoke scathingly of May as an infantile rebellion against paternal authority, without appearing to realise that this was precisely one of the most politically significant things about it. The politics of the family (as the fall of the Great Gallic Paterfamilias himself, General de Gaulle, in 1969 vividly illustrated) were henceforth unquestionably a major focus of conflict and discussion. There were many who, in the analyses and post-mortems that filled May 1978, took after the jaundiced and patronising tone of Aron's remarks ten years before. It was, after all, only a couple of months since the Left's resounding defeat in the parliamentary elections. This is almost certainly why the tenth anniversary was greeted in the French left-wing press with silence (*Les Temps Modernes* made no mention of it), or with anecdotal reminiscence (*Le Nouvel Observateur* interviewed a number of celebrated participants for their recollections). *La Nouvelle Critique* (theoretical journal of the PCF, so hostile to the events while they were in progress) significantly published an article by Armand Spire (commercial director of the Party's publishing house, Éditions Sociales) entitled 'Mai 68, mai 78: dix ans, ça suffit pas' ['May 68, May 78: ten years is not enough']. Spire there maintained that historians might well come to see May as the beginning of 'a progressive passage from the old capitalist regime to the new form of socialism whose outline was drawn by the Communists of France at their 22nd Party Congress'[7] – the Congress at which the concept of the dictatorship of the proletariat was officially removed from the Party's programme. The identification of the twin questions of power and desire as central to May was not a new one, but Spire's article marked one of the first occasions on which a Communist intellectual had acknowledged it in print. The *rapprochement* between old and new Left was, it would seem, just around the corner.

A different diagnosis was offered, in the May 1978 number of the journal *Esprit*, by Serge July, editor of the newspaper *Libération*. *Libération* started as a Leftist press-agency in 1971; began to appear as a newspaper (although rather sporadically) in 1973, under the patronage of Sartre; and has subsequently developed into a professionally-produced daily, clearly identified with the Left, though less strident than in its early days, and a byword in contemporary France for its 'courrier des lecteurs', a column of polymorphously perverse requests for correspondence, travelling-partners, and (above all) lovers from readers of the most diverse kinds. *Libération*, while not strictly an intellectual phenomenon, is produced and consumed by people who might be described as intellectuals, and its evolution from Maoist broadsheet to French 'alternative press' parallels some of the most important developments on the Left since 1968.

Régis Debray's 'Modest Contribution to the Rites and Ceremonies of the Tenth Anniversary' (referred to in English because of its ready, albeit condensed, availability in *New Left Review*), differed from both the 'political' interpretation of Spire and the 'cultural' one of July, who spoke of *Libération* as 'the paper in which the generation of '68 found a place and a style to express itself'.[8] Nobody could accuse Debray of facile nostalgia for the 'month of the barricades', which he had spent in a Bolivian prison because of his involvement with left-wing guerrilla activity. This, and his consistently strong commitment to the Parti Socialiste, mean that his reading deserves respect, however much one suspects it of having been designed to *épater le bourgeois*. Debray maintained that May was in fact the 'cradle of a new bourgeois society',[9] the pent-up explosion of social institutions that had lagged far behind the rate of industrial and technological advance, so that 'industrialisation had to be given a new morality, not because the poets were clamouring for a new one but because industry required it'. This version of (the) events is certainly given credibility by the dominance of the Giscardian over the Gaullist Right between Pompidou's death in 1974 and Mitterrand's victory in 1981. Giscard's style – a well-manicured amalgam of French patrician and transatlantic entrepreneur – figured his greater openness to American influence, cultural and political, and the dynamism which (befitting a graduate of the prestigious École Normale d'Administration) he strenuously brought to the office of President. In the wake of his triumph in March 1978, it was all too easy to believe, with Debray, that the May events had 'accomplished the opposite of what they intended'[10] – that, far from shaking off the oppressive yoke of industrial functionalism, they had paradoxically served to move French society into the industrial–functional era.

The most comprehensive taxonomy of interpretations of the events was in fact produced only two years after they had died down, by Philippe Béneton and Jean Touchard in the *Revue française de sociologie politique* (June 1970). The major commentaries to have appeared since (such as the three just dealt with) fit quite readily under one or more of Béneton and Touchard's eight headings, which indicates both how thorough their work was and how rapidly explanations and exegeses multiplied in the two years after May.

Béneton and Touchard's eight types of explanation are:

(1) that the events were an *enterprise of subversion* (a sophisticated way of blaming them on Reds under the bed);
(2) that they represented a *crisis in the university*, provoked by the

outdatedness of the institution and the lack of real contact between teachers and taught;

(3) that they were a *rush of blood to the head,* a revolt against the parental and paternalistic order;
(4) that they corresponded to a *spiritual crisis of contemporary civilisation;*
(5) that they *moved the class-struggle onto new ground,* through the prominence of the 'new social movements';
(6) that they were a *traditional social conflict* occurring at a time of high unemployment among the young;
(7) that they were a *political crisis* rooted in the inflexibility of institutions rather than in their unpopularity; and
(8) that they were a *chance concatenation of circumstances,* in which one thing led to another with no compelling overall pattern or design.

With the benefit of nearly seventeen years' hindsight, it is possible to say that Béneton and Touchard's types of explanation all contain varying degress of truth with the exception of (1), which is an inane calumny, and (8), which is likely to satisfy only devotees of the 'monkeys-on-typewriters' theory of creation. That the events would not have occurred if the university system had not been hopelessly outdated is hardly open to doubt; the 'rush-of-blood-to-the-head' version favoured by Raymond Aron has, as has already been suggested, important political implications; and, while Marxists might tend to recoil from any explanation of anything that includes the word 'spiritual', the exalted tone of Morin's writing (which appeared as a day-by-day chronicle in *Le Monde* of May 1968), and the important involvement of left-wing Christians, alike indicate that the events were a qualitatively new experience for those who took part in them. The 'traditional social conflict' clearly understates the importance of what happened, but is a salutary corrective to some of the over-charismatic views expressed under (4); and there was agreement across the political spectrum, from General de Gaulle and his new catchword 'participation' through to Debray's pessimistic analysis, that the ossification of French social and political institutions had lain at the root of the events.

It is not surprising that such a complex interweaving of diverse factors had such complex, and often asynchronous, effects on French intellectual life. The chapters that follow will endeavour to give an account of these in the historical and institutional context in which they arose, looking at work done specifically on the intellectual's role in post-

1968 France; at developments in (and recantations of) Marxist theory; at the specific importance of psychoanalysis and of the various feminist and libertarian politics that sprang up from or in opposition to it; at the political implications of the theoretical work of linguistic philosophy that has been influential over the past two decades; and at the heavily-marketed phenomenon of the 'new philosophers' and the significant revival of interest in sociology.

To see the 'spirit of May' as the First Cause of all these developments is tempting, but absurd; its very heterogeneity, and theirs, render such a reduction valueless. Rather than looking for 'causes' or 'influences' (both of which imply an idealistic or teleological view of history), the concern here will be to plot shifts in the intellectual configuration of post-1968 France and to see how these might illuminate, as they are illuminated by, wider political and institutional changes. First of all, however, we have to look at the disillusionment with the Left – among intellectuals and others – that at this distance seems almost to have set in with the first hangovers of the May 1981 rejoicings.

2 Disillusionment and the Role of the Intellectual in France

Those who expected May 1981 to be a 'second coming' of May 1968 were bound to be disappointed. The worldwide recession had led to a much harsher economic climate (and French intellectuals, however much the Marxists among them profess the determination of the economic in the last instance, have never as a group been particularly strong on economics); the heterogeneity of the social and political groupings that had combined to bring Mitterrand to power, unlike that of the movements active in May, was conducive to *realpolitik* rather than revolution; and all manner of problems to do with the complexity of French institutional structures presented themselves to the new regime in a way that could not simply be ignored. These factors affected the manner in which all sections of society judged the Socialist government, but there were others more specifically relevant to the French intelligentsia.

In the first place, much of the work that had gone on both before and after 1968 had been concerned with the various contradictory processes at work in capitalist society. The interplay or 'imbrication' (a common post-1968 'buzzword') of the political, the economic, and the ideological, or of the imaginary, the symbolic, and the real, that characterised respectively Althusser's reading of Marx and Lacan's reading of Freud, involved a highly sophisticated teasing-out of the different roles of different processes in different situations. As Denis Kambouchner had already pointed out in the 'tenth-anniversary' issue of the magazine *Autrement*, these theories seemed to represent 'all at once the *nec plus ultra* of intellectual rigour, the prospect of a living pedagogy, and the theoretical capital of the revolution' – a judgement relevant to earlier comments on the 'two Maos' and the *Tel Quel* declaration. There is no doubt that the articulation of Marxist and Freudian concepts produced some of the most exciting intellectual work to have gone on in Europe since the Second World War; but the other side to this was that, as Kambouchner points out, 'in no situation does Marxist or

Freudian thought hold out the prospect of any kind of immediate liberation'.[1]

Immediate liberation was precisely what many had felt to be just around the corner in May 1968; and the intellectual stress on the complexity and contradictoriness of process, like the multiple structural problems by which the new Socialist regime was assailed, had a dampening and discouraging effect on the 'utopian' heritage of the events. Much more apparent as a source of dissatisfaction, however, were political developments outside France. Mao's reputation as the 'Great Helmsman' was shattered by the revelations about the Cultural Revolution. (Interestingly, it was *Libération*, self-styled lodestar of the post-'68 generation, that helped to draw widespread attention to these in 1976.) The euphoria caused by the ending of the Vietnam War seemed to become a nightmare with the ensuing bloodbath and the horrors of the Pol Pot regime in Cambodia. Many on the French Left felt doubly compromised by these, for while what was then 'Indo-China' had been under French colonial occupation many of the Cambodian leaders had been learning their Marxism in Paris. The PCF's attempts at self-rehabilitation were drained of their credibility by the Party's timorousness in condemning Soviet or Soviet-backed repression first in Afghanistan, then in Poland. It is important to try to account for the shell-shocked, and often highly unanalytical, way in which many hitherto left-wing intellectuals responded to this litany of Marxist disasters and malpractices. Philippe Sollers, moving spirit behind the June 1968 'manifesto', proclaimed his affinity with American freedom and diversity, and is widely believed to have voted for Giscard in 1981. A spiritualised form of condemnation usurped any serious political analysis in the discourse of such as the 'new philosophers'; one-time rigorous ideologues simply threw their spiritual hands up in horror.

This can be seen as a telling indication of how deep their Leftist commitment had really been, or of their *naïveté* in investing their hopes for liberation and revolution in successive 'Socialist fatherlands' that were largely imaginary constructs. But it also has to do with the nightmarish inversion of many of the concepts developed on the intellectual Left over the years – now suddenly turned against their advocates. Solzhenitsyn's *The Gulag Archipelago* had not merely repeated what everybody on the Left knew about Stalin's Russia, it had revealed a new dimension of horror by showing how the victims themselves came to acquiesce in their own oppression (and often liquidation). This struck a chord with much of the work that had been going on around notions of the materiality of language and the importance of signifying practice; here was a grisly illustration of how deep the political and ideological effects of language, in its most basic form of self-denomination, could run. Likewise, the orthodox international Communist line on Soviet dissidents (that they were punished not for what they thought and said, but for what they *did* to harm 'Socialist society') was difficult to maintain in the light of such work. For *Tel Quel* and others, to say something, because of what Lacan terms 'the materiality of the signifier', was actually – literally – to 'do' something. The Kremlin's distinction seemed untenable.

The discrediting of Mao was in some ways an even more severe blow. It was not only as a wall-poster icon that he had been important for the French Left; Althusser's rereading of Marx (especially the essay *Contradiction et surdétermination* [*Contradiction and overdetermination*]) had drawn extensively on Mao's philosophical essay *On Contradiction*, so that his influence stretched beyond the far Left into the PCF intelligentsia. Charles Reeve's *Paper Tiger*, a work which presented China as still a fundamentally capitalist society, was published in France in 1972; to quote Serge Quadruppani in *Catalogue du prêt-à-penser français depuis 1968* [*Catalogue of ready-made French ideas since 1968*]:

> In 1972, in France, the Maoist lie was not merely endorsed by a few hotheads in the Gauche prolétarienne [extreme 'spontaieist' Maoist grouping] and a few dogmatists from *L'humanité rouge* [daily paper of the 'Mao-Stalinist' party (PCFML) in the aftermath of the 1966 expulsions] or *Tel Quel.* The great majority of left-wing intellectuals were still taken in by the grisly farce of the Cultural Revolution. Thus, Reeve's work, whose analyses all subsequently turned out to be correct, was greeted with a few kind words in *Annales,* a specialist journal, and a contemptuous short article by Patrice de Beer in *Le Monde.*[2]

Thus it was that, more than two years later, *Tel Quel* was still able to dispatch its elite corps – Sollers, Kristeva, Roland Barthes, François Wahl, and Marcelin Pleynet – on a tour of China enthusiastically written up in the autumn issue. Quadruppani draws an embarrassing parallel between this and the similar journeys undertaken by such figures as André Gide to the USSR when that was still thought to provide a model for socialism. The close integration of political discourse and the practical details of everyday life in shipyards and collective farms was praised to the skies, and the assertion that hunger and illiteracy had virtually been done away with was accepted uncritically, despite evidence to the contrary.

The importance of Mao's philosophical writings is not necessarily negated by later revelations about his career, but this did not prevent the French intelligentsia from dropping him like a hot brick. It has often been observed that the Oriental country which now holds the most fascination for the French is not Communist China, but the Japan of high-technology capitalism, with its negligible record of strikes and carefully-integrated work-force. (Roland Barthes had been the first leading French intellectual to show an interest in Japanese society, in his *L'empire des signes* [*The empire of signs*] of 1970.) We shall see that many of the 'new philosophers' had previously been (or at least called themselves) Maoists; their retreat into a spiritual discourse evacuated of any analytical political content can be understood as a response to the traumatic revelations about their former hero. The specifically political influence of the Leftist intelligentsia during the 1960s and 1970s was minimal. While the majority of new concepts and the prevailing intellectual orthodoxy were clearly of the Left, there was little connection between this and the nuts-and-bolts of day-to-day activity; a point graphically illustrated by the fact that, while the roll-call of (past or present) PCF intellectuals is an impressive one, there is no comparable phenomenon in the Socialist Party, which now dominates French left-wing institutional life. Daniel Lindenberg points out:

> The debolshevisation of the intelligentsia was able to take successively the forms of a revival of 'Western Marxism', the transitional crystal-lisation of *gauchisme*, a sudden breakthrough of the anti-totalitarian imperative, it could one by one fertilise the expanding ranks of social and human scientists, provide the Fifth Republic with top-quality executives, bring back to the Churches a good many lost sheep, and multiply tenfold the solvent demand for a new kind of psychoanalytic institution; but its effect on the properly institutional aspect of the revival of socialism in France, perceptible at the electoral level since 1967 and organisationally since 1971, was non-existent.'[3]

This may well be another reason why disillusionment was so quick to set in after May 1981; the link between left-wing intellectual activity and the Socialist triumph was not a self-evident one, and it may have been difficult for intellectuals to think of the Mitterrand regime as 'theirs', particularly given the problems into which the new government almost immediately ran. Academics are perhaps more likely to vote for socialist parties simply because they tend to be more generous with resources, and this is compounded in France by other, more specific factors. These include the effects of 1789 and the Dreyfus Affair already referred to, the Napoleonic heritage of competitive examinations and *grandes écoles*, providing a series of meritocratic paths for upward social mobility, and the long-standing tradition of radical anti-clericalism among schoolteachers – stretching from the institution of free, compulsory secular education in 1881 through to the controversial, and ultimately discarded, 1984 attempt to integrate denominational schools with the State system.

Not all those intellectuals whose sympathies lay with the Left supported Mitterrand at the first ballot in 1981, for many were attracted by the facetious candidacy of the comedian Coluche, standing on a platform of apolitical nihilism. Pierre Bourdieu and Gilles Deleuze were among the major intellectuals to declare their support for him – another indication perhaps of how divorced Leftist intellectual activity can become from the realities of political power. The Socialist Party's most prominent intellectual is currently Régis Debray, now one of Mitterrand's political advisers. In *Le Nouvel Observateur* of 29 April 1974, he summarises the reasons why he felt France to be ripe for socialism:

> A long feudal tradition, Catholic influence, the bourgeois revolution already a long way off, the slow constitution of hostile classes, the fusion of class and class-consciousness in a labour movement with its own vision of the world, the special place of intelligence and intellectuals in the social imaginary ('France, the country of ideas', as Marx said); here is a backlog, so to speak, which forces us to move forward.[4]

It was immediately before the 'move forward' Debray predicted that he produced his most significant work on 'the special place of intelligence and intellectuals in the social imaginary': *Le pouvoir intellectuel en France* [*Intellectual power in France*] (1979) and *Le Scribe* [*The Scribe*] (1980). *Le pouvoir intellectuel* is an indispensable text for under-standing the place – in two senses of the word – of intellectuals in contemporary France: not only the position of influence they occupy, but the different points within the social formation at which this influence makes itself felt. Debray's main thesis is that what he calls the 'upper intelligentsia' have sought to maintain their elite status by moving from one site of symbolic power to another as the social formation has changed and developed. University education expanded considerably between 1930 and 1977, in which year there were 41 905 university lecturers in France; Debray sees this as the main structural reason why from the 1920s the 'upper intelligentsia' devoted more of their time and energy to work for publishing-houses. The more higher education expanded, the more restricted each individual lecturer's audience was clearly likely to be, and thus the greater the incentive for the ambitious to try to commandeer sites more difficult of access.

1968, for Debray, is another similar watershed, when the focus moved from the world of publishing to that of the media:

> In May '68, for the first time, the media *made* history directly, the fate of the country was decided on the radio and acted out on television. May '68 is the point at which the observer looking back through his binoculars can exclaim: Nothing in intellectual society will ever again be as it used to! If Gide in 1936 has a conversation in the street with Marceau-Pivert, the news-value comes from Gide. When Aragon talks to Cohn-Bendit in 1968, it comes from Cohn-Bendit.[5]

If Debray is appalled by the emergence of the intellectual 'media-celebrity', this is not purely for ethical reasons such as underlie the Leavisite attacks on mass-culture in Britain. He sees the phenomenon as *politically* disastrous – in the elitist cliques to which it gives rise, the self-preening narcissism of the self-selected 'creators' (Sollers is represented by a repellently individualistic attack on writers' trade unions), and the implicit market-economic logic that underpins it. The lifting of price-controls on books and the emergence of large-scale literary and cultural 'warehouses' such as the FNAC, purveying books and records along with other consumer goods under one roof at greatly reduced prices, was a parallel phenomenon. It might have seemed that this would make 'culture' (however defined) more freely accessible to the 'masses' (whoever they might be); but the result was in fact to increase the intensive marketing of a select few authors who could be relied upon to sell rapidly, and the Mitterrand Government was not slow to reimpose price-controls in this field. Debray does not mention the 'FNAC phenomenon', but it clearly forms part of the institutional context for his criticism of the simultaneous proliferation and concentration of intellectual power:

We can see the university world, and the wider intellectual world, abandon *its own logic of organisation, selection, and reproduction,* to adopt the market logic inherent in the working of the media. For the intellectual, dependence on the State has never been an ideal; to depend on the market of opinion, and thus on a commercial plebiscite, for one's ethical and intellectual validation may well turn out to be a nightmare.[6]

The political thrust of this riposte to the 'new philosophers' and to the wider implications of liberal cultural philosophy is clear. Debray has less to say about individual names and institutions (no doubt because he did not wish to play the media-celebrity game), but one personality on whom he focuses is worthy of attention. This is Bernard Pivot, presenter of the weekly television-programme *Apostrophes* and editor of the magazine *Lire* (a spin-off from *Apostrophes*). The programme brings together a number of writers each week to discuss (and thus to promote) their latest books. An appearance is thus highly coveted among French writers and intellectuals, and it would seem that much intriguing and string-pulling can be necessary to secure one.

What is interesting about Pivot from our point of view is not only the concentration of intellectual power in his hands (certainly unparallelled by any individual in British society), but the way in which he has been able, first on television and then in print, to reach a widespread public with a literary and intellectual programme. For Debray, his influence on intellectual life is a pernicious one, for he fits clearly into the category of 'diffusers of thought', whose increasing dominance over the producers is at the heart of the problem. Hervé Hamon and Patrick Rotman in *Les Intellocrates* [*The 'Intellocrats'*], on the other hand, adopt a less harshly critical view. They point out that many of those who appear *chez* Pivot have up to then been relatively little-known, which suggests that he has a certain democratising influence. This is borne out by his unglamorous formal education (his highest qualification is a diploma in journalism), and well-publicised recreational tastes. His passions are watching football and the pursuit of gastronomy, especially that of the Beaujolais region where he has a house, so it is not difficult to see how he can act as a bridge between the intelligentsia and the general public.

There can be no doubt that the concentraion of symbolic power in Pivot's hands is symptomatic of the intellectual shift towards a media-based oligarchy. Hamon and Rotman's book is a wittily scurrilous anatomy of the part played in this by the various Left Bank intellectual 'mafias' – the name-naming counterpart to Debray's historical analysis. They stress the closeness and variety of the institutional links within the Parisian intellectual world: educational (the importance of the École Normale Supérieure and the *khâgnes* preparatory classes at the major *lycées*), political (ex-Communists, radical Catholics, *soixante-huitards*), and journalistic. Thus, *Le Nouvel Observateur* is singled out as the major 'talent-spotting' journal drawing upon young academics who, 'though equipped with the indispensable open-sesame [the *agrégation*], have no inclination to follow the ritual course of the thesis'.[7]

This, like much of what Debray says about the movement of intellectual investment from universities into publishing and the media, illustrates how the structure of the French academic system affects the types of career open to its members. To secure a high-school teacher's or lecturer's salary, it is normally necessary to pass a competitive examination (the *agrégation*), success or failure in which depends on how many vacancies and new posts in one's field arise in a particular academic year. It was customary for university teachers, once duly *agrégé(e)*, to go on to prepare a *doctorat d'état* – a lengthy thesis, automatically published upon approval, which was a necessary, but not a sufficient, condition for professorial advancement. The length of time such a thesis generally took, and the drying-up of posts above the *maître-assistant* (or 'career lecturer') grade, have led to disillusionment with this type of career-structure; even regulations requiring newly-appointed lecturers to complete a certain portion of their doctorate within a few years of appointment or face demotion to a high-school post have not altogether turned the tide. The tendency now is for the aspirant intellectual celebrity to seek to combine university teaching with journalistic and (if s/he is sufficiently well-connected) radio and television appearances, producing pamphlets and articles which bring in money and enable their author to live in Paris, rather than theses which are read by nobody and can no longer even guarantee advancement within the most modest provincial faculty.

Again, the hegemony of Paris is an all-important factor here. Even New York is not quite so unquestionably dominant, for the Californian metropolises of Los Angeles and San Francisco provide an alternative cultural focus. A great many lecturers at French provincial universities – far more than their British counterparts – choose to live in the capital, group their classes together on two or three days a week, and commute or take a room for the night. This is partly because many of the universities within commuting reach of Paris (Rouen, Amiens,

Reims . . .) are of recent foundation, so that there is not the university-city tradition classically associated with Oxford and Cambridge; but that in its turn is determined by the prominence of Paris. Paris is where virtually all leading French intellectuals receive their education, and the homing instinct, reinforced by the cultural and administrative centralisation already referred to, is responsible for the major single difference between French and Anglo-American intellectual life.

Debray criticises the French intellectual world from a clearly left-wing perspective, and the work of Hamon and Rotman (the latter a one-time Trotskyist militant) is similarly informed. But there has also been much criticism of the 'Left Bank world' from less radical perspectives. François Bourricaud, in *Le Bricolage Idéologique* [*Ideological 'Do-it-yourself'*], pillories many left-wing thinkers for what he sees as their unwarranted appropriation of scientific vocabulary. For Bourricaud, 'intellectuals are specialists in ideological debate, and since ideological debate, bearing in mind the kind of objects with which it deals, is only very distantly related to true scientific discussion, intellectuals are condemned to "do-it-yourself" '.[8] The use of the term *bricolage* derives from Lévi-Strauss's distinction between the intellectual 'engineer', who devises and applies new concepts, and the 'do-it-yourself' person or *bricoleur*, who uses already-existing concepts, selecting and discarding as appropriate. Bourricaud argues that the besetting vice of the French intellectual world consists in its attempt to deny the inevitability of *bricolage* and its promotion of approximations and recycled notions as if they had a scientific validity. This is obviously more applicable to the Left than to the Right, if only because of Marxism's self-proclaimed status as 'scientific socialism'; Bourricaud maintains in his final chapter that 'the ideology of the Right is largely *dominated* in that it responds to the Left, which is the first to speak'.[9]

Bourricaud's theses have much in common with those of his colleague Raymond Boudon, whose article 'L'intellectuel et ses publics: les singularités françaises' ['The intellectual and his audiences: French particularities'], in the Documentation Française collection of essays *Français, qui êtes-vous?* [*French people, who are you?*], analyses the particular structures of the French intellectual market. Boudon identifies three types of market for intellectual products: type I, a specialist market of intellectual peers; type II, the wider educated public, grouped around such publications as *Le Monde* and *Le Nouvel Observateur*; and type III, the more diffuse 'general' market, obviously much influenced by Pivot. He detects (and, implicitly at least, deplores) a movement away from the first type of market, which he relates back to

May 1968 in two important ways. In the first place, he claims that the more uniform career-structure that the teaching unions were able to secure as part of the university reforms has diminished institutional incentives to produce specialised, 'type I' work – a dubious argument if only because it comes close to implying that such work, before 1968, automatically guaranteed promotion. Secondly, the anarchistic side of May – its ebulliently iconoclastic attitude towards established academic specialisms and divisions – has for Boudon left an enduring imprint upon French intellectual life: 'Consequently, an "anarchistic" epistemology is able to develop and legitimise a production which rests on aesthetic rather than cognitive criteria, even when it puts itself forward as "scientific" (the case of Roland Barthes's semiology is significant in this respect)'.[10]

This is quite literally a reactionary argument, imbued with nostalgia for the rigidity of pre-1968 days, and utopian to boot in its desire to put the clock back. But the bizarre amalgam of conceptual rigour and free-wheeling textuality we have seen at work in the *Tel Quel* 'manifesto' has clearly left its mark, in the erosion of established disciplinary boundaries and the consequent calling into question of specialist competence, if not in the polysemic 'Grand Science' which was the dream to which it aspired.

All the work looked at in this chapter accords prominence to the role of the intellectual in political life, and it is this that Debray analyses in *Le Scribe*. Marx was keenly aware of how important ideas have always been in French society, though as Debray emphasises his work leaves no place for specific treatment of the role of the intellectual – a species that would disappear under Communism along with the distinction between mental and manual labour. (It is noteworthy in this connection that Cuba and China both attached a great deal of importance to the abolition of this distinction, a position which won them a good many friends at one time in the Western intelligentsia.) For Debray, the political and the religious are coextensive rather than radically separate, as is shown by his description of Marxism as 'the sacred afterword to a critical enterprise'.[11] Both spheres, in France, have the task of producing 'ecclesiastical' or general concepts (as it might be 'universals') and this helps us to under-stand why the university grew out of (and away from) the Church (the Sorbonne was originally a religious foundation).

Debray refers to Michel Foucault's concept of *enfermement* or 'shutting-away', developed in *Histoire de la Folie* [*History of Madness*] and *Naissance de la Clinique* [*Birth of the Clinic*], as an example of a notion that originated in a specialised intellectual field but very swiftly moved outside, to become a general (and often overused) byword. Unlike Boudon, Debray does not necessarily deprecate this tendency; rather, he sees it as the necessary condition for the intellectuals' access to political power. 'In what country, at what period has there been a social revolution – bourgeois or socialist – when the "laity" and the "clergy" have been divided?'; the question is a purely rhetorical one. The importance of intellectuals for Marxism on the one hand and the political and institutional life of France on the other is clearly proven by Debray's analysis, whose proximity to the Socialist electoral victory is one of the best proofs that: 'A State needs discourses to keep itself going just as its enemies do to overthrow it.'[12]

3   Intellectuals and Marxism Since 1968 – Sartre

By no means all the work that has gone on on the French Left in recent years can be described, or would describe itself, as 'Marxist'. Thinkers such as Barthes or Lacan have been thus labelled in print, on evidence seemingly no more substantial than the former's denunciation of the *Mythologies* of bourgeois consumerism, and the latter's influence on and affinities with the May movements and the ideas of Althusser. There are those, like Foucault or Deleuze, who have explicitly rejected the application of the term to their work while still clearly committed to the Left, and those, of whom Derrida is the best-known example, who would lay claim to Marxist sympathies not unequivocally apparent in what they write. And the numerous 'alternative politics' that sprang out of May have often defined themselves precisely in opposition to the monolithic centralism characteristic of much French Marxist thought.

This was most marked during the Stalinist era, when Stalin's own highly simplistic version of Marxist philosophy dominated intellectual life in the PCF. Michael Kelly points out in *Modern French Marxism* that this was in some ways appropriate to the beleaguered political position of the Party at the time; it may also have been at least in part responsible for it. The haemorrhage of members after the invasion of Hungary in 1956 and Khruschev's revelations at the Soviet Party Congress that same year, and the Party's willingness to vote for an increased 'defence' budget to carry on the Algerian War, are of a piece with its expulsion of Henri Lefebvre, one of its leading intellectuals, two years later. History in a manner of speaking repeated itself after 1968; the Party's membership declined as a result first of its attitude towards the May events, then of the Soviet invasion of Czechoslovakia, and two years later Roger Garaudy, with Althusser the Party's most prominent intellectual at the time, was expelled.

Despite this sorry record, the PCF has remained the focal point of debate on the Marxist Left in France since the Second World War. The Socialist Party, apart from being a relative newcomer, does not style itself

'Marxist', and thus does not have the same programmatic commitment to the elaboration and application of theory; and the major intellectual figures in the smaller groups (such as Alain Krivine, Trotskyist historian and General Secretary of the LCR) have tended to channel much of their energies into day-to-day political work. PCF members, ex-members, or sympathisers form the largest bloc during our period.

Sartre, of course, never held a Party card, and even in his fellow-travelling period never voted in an election. By 1968 he had moved to what the Party disparagingly calls an 'ultra-left' position, working closely with Maoist groups in particular. In *Situations X*, a compilation of political and autobiographical texts dating from between 1971 and 1976, he accuses the PCF of having broken the alliance between the intelligentsia and the proletariat which was widespread in the nineteenth century. It seems almost as though Sartre in this period set himself single-handedly the task of reconstituting that link. The polarisation of his activity has been much commented upon: on the one hand, involvement with the banned Maoist newspaper *La Cause du Peuple*, and subsequently with *Libération*, participation in demonstrations, and attempts to get himself arrested, shrewdly rebutted by the regime; on the other, single-minded intellectual concentration on his immense psycho-biographical study of Flaubert, *L'Idiot de la Famille* [*The Idiot of the Family*].

An interview in *Situations X* makes it plain that for Sartre *L'Idiot de la Famille* was a political work, a 'settling of accounts . . . with all families'.[1] It can certainly be argued that Sartre's major influence on French society and within the West as a whole has been exerted not so much through his petition-signing activities and commitment to Marxism as through the radical alternative his way of life offered to the nuclear family – that it was the Simone de Beauvoir and Sartre of St-Germain-des-Prés rather than of the revolutionary Left that had the greater social impact. In this light, it is possible to see *L'Idiot de la Famille* as the development and extension of political 'work in progress', and we shall see in Chapter 6 that Simone de Beauvoir's feminist evolution complements and corroborates this. The title of Lenin's major work on the political role of the intellectuals – *What is to be Done?* – could serve as an epigraph for Sartre's unceasing questioning, of himself and others, throughout his life. In *Plaidoyer pour les Intellectuels* [*A Plea for the Intellectuals*], a series of lectures given in Japan in 1966 and published in France in 1972, he develops the notion that the intellectual is precisely the person who 'does not mind their own business' – that s/he is animated by the contradiction between the pursuit of truth-in-practice and the values of the dominant ideology. The 1972 preface to this effectively excludes any other way of pursuing this contradiction than by abdicating the classic intellectual role in order to 'serve the people' – a key Maoist slogan. Sartre had already demonstrated his attachment to this principle by his activity in May 1968, spending a night on the barricades and interviewing Daniel Cohn-Bendit as if Cohn-Bendit were the more famous of the two (which indeed, according to Debray, he was). From being famous for being Sartre, the curse that had dogged him for years, it was as though he were moving towards 'un-being Sartre'. *Les Maos en France* [*The Maoists in France*], one of the interviews collected in *Situations X*, bears this out strikingly. It begins with a disclaimer; Sartre is not a Maoist (any more, presumably, than he ever was a Communist). He is a friend and collaborator of theirs, presenting their views and ideas to the general public (the text appeared as the preface to a book of interviews with Maoist militants). The three characteristics that most particularly strike Sartre as politically desirable are their espousal of violence ('A socialist cannot but be violent, for his goal is one that the ruling class utterly repudiates');[2] their spontaneism, which puts them into contact with that 'popular memory' later to be dissected by Michel Foucault; and their anti-authoritarian morality.

What is striking here is the manner in which Sartre subordinates himself to the Maoists, using his prestige to amplify and propagate their ideas rather than ideas he has himself developed. The stress on morality as a cornerstone of political action has much in common with the earlier Sartre's denunciation of the bad faith that is an inevitable corollary of being a bourgeois, as with the view of Third World writers such as Franz Fanon that violence is the necessary morality of the oppressed. This strand is not particularly prominent in post-Sartrean left-wing thought in France; the stress on the scientificity of Marxism and psychoanalysis, and the importance attached to forces or structures that go beyond the ethically autonomous individual, have all but usurped the place previously accorded to the morality of politics. *Les Maos en France* thus appears doubly dated, in its discourse as well as in the political example it proposes.

But the long-term failure of the Maoists' tactics in France makes it easy to forget how radical a challenge they posed to the established social and political order. The better-educated militants were sent into industry, to build mass support; they were known as *établis*, which means both 'a settled or established person' and 'a workbench'. There was no bourgeois nonsense about the pursuit of a career or the specific role of the intellectual – 'serving the people' was what counted, and in this sense it is tempting (especially as many of them came from well-off Catholic families) to see the *établis* as latter-day mendicant friars of the shop-floor. Clearly this strategy no longer made sense when the recession set in; even unskilled manual jobs were not always easy to come by, and intellectuals were reluctant to drop out of a bourgeois career they might never be able to drop back into. In this respect, the Maoist strategy can be seen as rooted in relative affluence.

Maoist militants did not confine their industrial intervention to conventional forms of trade-union activity. Sequestrations, hostage-taking, and other forms of guerrilla action were frequent, and *Les Temps Modernes* enthusiastically endorsed these. Sartre, meanwhile, frankly accepted his own contradictions, as a particularly privileged bourgeois who chose to put his privilege and influence at the service of 'the people', and was thus able to protect *La Cause du Peuple* so that it could still appear when it was officially banned and two of its leaders were in prison.

The most illuminating of the interventions made during our period by Sartre and *Les Temps Modernes* was in the so-called 'Bruay affair'. This erupted in April 1972, when the body of a sixteen-year-old girl, Brigitte Dewevre, was discovered on some waste-ground in the small mining-town of Bruay in North-Eastern France. Suspicion fell upon a wealthy local lawyer, Leroy, and the absence of the type of reporting restrictions imposed by the British laws of libel and contempt of court led to a welter of speculation and extensive background material of a kind that in Britain normally emerges only after a trial. The Artois area (where Bruay is situated) is a coal-mining one, where incomes are low and families often live crowded into back-to-back houses. Leroy (who acted as solicitor for the leading colliery owners) lived a life of considerable ease amid all this hardship, and it was his life-style and social associations rather than the evidence linking him with the crime (which, although copious, was largely circumstantial) that drew down on him the ire of much of the extreme Left. His consumption of steak and seafood, his luxurious house in Bruay, his second home on the coast were all lavishly documented in the popular press rather than in *Le Monde*, whose would-be dignified reticence met with scorn in *La Cause du Peuple*. When, in a further Zolaesque twist, a working-class youth arrested after confessing to the killing was released after admitting that he had done so only out of bravado, the stage was finally set for a journalistic show-trial in which the class bias of French justice and French society were to be vehemently denounced.

One peculiarity of the French judicial system is that, before charges are brought, an examining magistrate is dispatched to inquire into the case and determine whether there is sufficient evidence for a trial to take place. The magistrate assigned to the Bruay case, Maître Pascal, seemed from the first convinced of the case against Leroy, and his robustly populist approach set against Leroy's patrician *hauteur* seemed to epitomise the conflict between two classes and two conceptions of justice. The PCF was critical of his approach; *Les Temps Modernes*, on the other hand, in the special issue it devoted to the Bruay affair, said: 'Behind Pascal, the bourgeoisie feels and knows that there is the people, and that is just what they do not want.'[3]

Yet another disturbing dimension to the affair was provided by suggestions of so-called sexual 'aberrancy' on Leroy's part. Although in his forties, he had never married, had a fiancée with whom his relations seemed unfashionably distant and courteous, and was alleged to have taken part in sadistic practices with prostitutes. The fact that Brigitte Dewevre's breasts had been mutilated (though there had been no sexual penetration), and that five other working-class girls were reputed to have been killed over a period in the area, was taken in some quarters as a conclusive indictment of Leroy. The reasons why the popular press dwelt on certain of these details were obviously very different from those of *Les Temps Modernes* or *La Cause du Peuple*; but there was a general suggestion that Leroy's role as wealthy bachelor representative of the ruling class ought to be sufficient to condemn him out of hand.

A whole panoply of 'alternative justice', inconceivable in Britain, was set in train by Maoist militants among the miners and in Paris; Sartre, Foucault, and others paid visits to Bruay. *Les Temps Modernes* quoted an old lady as saying that the crime must have been committed by a bourgeois, for a worker's crime would have been 'more emotional', and the sweeping extension of the case to the arraignment of an entire class is captured in these pages from the article 'Bruay is angry':

The bourgeoisie *can* and *will* massacre. It massacres every day, and the workers who catch the Paris metro early in the morning, or the girls who take the bus at the same time for the textile factories of Lille, do indeed look like living dead.

Yes, the bourgeoisie treats the workers like cattle, but that does not mean that any and every bourgeois will slaughter a young working-class girl . . . . The scorn they feel for the people they exploit comes a long way before their concern for justice.[4]

The inevitable result of the host of allegations and counter-allegations surrounding the affair was that the case never came to trial – a moral victory for either side, depending on whether one preferred to believe that there really was insufficient evidence against Leroy or that the bourgeois conspiracy of silence masquerading as 'justice' had finally prevailed. The idea of 'popular tribunals' to try matters of class-justice in parallel with the official judicial process had merely brought about a confusion of the issues.

The politics of *La Cause du Peuple* now appears as the furthest development of the 'maximalist' side of 1968, a stance figured in Sartre's article 'Élections, piège à cons' ['Elections, a trap for idiots'] of June 1973. The argument here rests on Sartre's concept of 'seriality' – the process by which bourgeois society renders human beings anonymous, confining them in functions that separate them from one another and thus rendering the formation of groups (as opposed to series) impossible. 'Seriality', while related to the more widespread concept of 'alienation', differs from it in that it does not presuppose some fundamental human essence from which individuals become separated. It points metonymically to the replacement of names by numbers, the interchangeability of humans one with another, rather than metaphorically to their estrangement from themselves. It is on this basis that Sartre affirms that 'when I vote, I abdicate my power . . . and I affirm that we, the voters, are always other than ourselves and that none of us can in any circumstances move from seriality to the group, except through the mediation of other people'.[5]

From a stimulating formulation of one of the major problems in advanced capitalist society, Sartre draws a political conclusion that can logically lead only to an individualism verging on the nihilistic or to all-or-nothing revolution. The latter is clearly designated by the text ('the Revolution will be drowned in the ballot-boxes, which is not surprising since that is what they are there for')[6]; the former, to judge by the exceptionally high number of Maoists who have left politics altogether, is perhaps more clearly figured by it.

That Sartre in his declining years came to speak of himself as no longer a Marxist did not necessarily imply a move to the right. Even his reconciliation with his *frère ennemi*, Raymond Aron, when both went to the Élysée to plead the cause of the Vietnamese 'boat people', betokened more a shift of traditional 'Left/Right' dividing lines than an ideological volte-face on Sartre's part. The 'Marxism' of the late texts is in reality of a highly eccentric kind, reposing upon a sweeping division between 'the bourgeoisie' and 'the masses' that in some ways goes right back to *La Nausée* [*Nausea*] (cf. the scene where Roquentin walks round the art-gallery in Bouville apostrophising the portraits of the bourgeoisie as 'bastards'). It was the shared loathing of the bourgeoisie from which both men came that finally led Sartre to feel much in common with Flaubert, and that same loathing imbued the political ethics that remain his most abiding social legacy.

It also, however, led to major flaws in his more overtly political work, exemplified by the attitude towards the Bruay affair – the grotesque conflation of personal and political exemplified in the question posed about Leroy's erotic habits 'Is there a class sexuality?'; the promotion of 'popular justice' against 'bourgeois justice' as though there were no possible scope for progressive intervention in the latter; above all, the widespread lumping-together, under the heading of 'the masses' or 'the people', of widely disparate social groupings. Of detailed analysis of changes in the class-structure and social balance of contemporary France, there was, beneath the 'street theatre' of popular trials and sequestered managing-directors, disturbingly little. The divisions among, and weakness of, the 'conventional' Left so scorned by *La Cause du Peuple* certainly made the conquest of power by conventional means seem impossibly distant; but, within that impossible distance, the work of the groupings around Sartre now appears the most impossibilist of all.

4 Intellectuals and Marxism Since 1968 – the Structuralists

The dominant strand in French Marxism from the early sixties, for some fifteen years, was so-called 'structuralist Marxism', whose best-known proponents were Louis Althusser and Nicos Poulantzas. This has been voluminously written about in English, and there would be little point in simply parrotting existing accounts. Emphasis will fall rather on the context in which this work was carried on, and the reasons why the PCF was such a favourable terrain for Althusser's brand of Marxism. The main reason is, in a nutshell, that that approach ran counter to all the other major tendencies within the Party at the time. So low was its stock, politically and intellectually, that the best hopes of renewal seemed to lie in a decisive rejection of its hitherto dominant trends – an 'epistemological break', indeed, of the kind that Althusser (whose former philosophy teacher Gaston Bachelard had coined the term) saw between the younger and the later Marx. Jean-Pierre Cotten, in *La Pensée de Louis Althusser* [*The Thought of Louis Althusser*], resumes the political factors that influenced the reception of Althusser's early major work (*Pour Marx* and *Lire le Capital*):

> ... an abrupt fall-out of the energy that had been mobilised against colonial violence, as if in a situation where there was no serious crisis on the horizon, where the symptoms of a new economic crisis were not yet perceptible, where there was relative economic growth, all that was left for 'left-wing intellectuals' was the temptation of revolutionary exoticism or the 'detour' through theory, a detour which could easily become an end in itself .... History, in France, seemed to have stopped; the fact that Marxism could then be remodelled through endless 'readings' is connected with the state of the class-struggle in France during this period.[1]

It was also connected with the Party's need to regain the intellectual credibility it had lost as a result of the revelations about the USSR and the mechanical sterility of the Stalinist years. It was the 'humanist' view of Marxism that tended to prevail as the major alternative to Stalinist materialism. Sartrean existentialism was an important current here, perhaps more in *informing* commitment to Marxism than in forming it; as we have seen, its stress on ethical self-questioning and the rejection of bourgeois values did not translate easily into party-political terms. More significant was the revival of interest in Hegel after the Second World War, under the aegis of the philosophers Alexandre Kojève and Jean Hyppolite. It was Hegel's notion of the dialectic that had served as the pre-text for Marx, and his articulation of what Michael Kelly calls 'a subjective dialectic of consciousness . . . [and] . . . an objective dialectic of nature and history'[2] was a major influence upon French Marxists and others during the post-war period.

Althusser's work was in sharp opposition alike to old-style Stalinism, Hegelian Marxism, and the Marxist humanisms expounded within the PCF by Roger Garaudy. The preface to *Pour Marx*, in which he situates his work in the aftermath of the period of 'philosophical dogmatism', served to distance him from Stalinism in its unreconstructed variety at least. He insisted in the essays in that work on the radical transformation Marx had wrought upon the Hegelian dialectic – not turning it upside-down so that material being determined human consciousness rather than vice versa, but remodelling it to give a far more many-layered account of the processes of social contradiction, and thereby according a degree of 'relative autonomy' to the spheres of the political, the economic, and the ideological across which human social activity inscribes itself.

It was in 1966 that Althusser engaged in a public debate with Roger Garaudy, on the theme of humanism in the PCF. Garaudy described Marxism as 'theoretical and practical humanism', warned of the dangers of confusing Marxist humanism with bourgeois individualism, and spoke of human beings as the subjects of history. Althusser retorted that 'humanism' was not a satisfactory theoretical concept, and that to link it with economism (understood as the pursuit of growth under a socialist regime, the pursuit of economic demands above all others under capitalism) would inevitably lead to the evasion of such key questions as the relations of production and the class-struggle – a theme to which he was to return seven years later in *Réponse à John Lewis* [*Reply to John Lewis*].

This debate set the tone for the major philosophical and political oppositions that were to structure the intellectual life of the PCF for the next decade at least. The intellectual, if not necessarily the political, debate increasingly went the way of the anti-humanists or 'structuralists', helped by Garaudy's expulsion in 1970. Althusser's own work, in the seventies in particular, moved from the theoretical sophistication of his early writings to a more polemical and interventionist tone – in Raymond Boudon's terms, from a 'type I' to a 'type III' intellectual market. This came about in response to the number and intensity of crises (both ideological and political) within the PCF over this period, so that Althusser's practice as writer and intellectual gave the lie to suggestions that he was interested only in the elaboration of increasingly recondite theoretical models.

It was with the insertion of theory into practice, and more especially of the anti-humanist Marxist theory he had developed into the French political practice of the time, that Althusser's work from 1968 through to the brutal interruption (or termination?) of his writing career in 1980, was above all concerned. His office at the École Normale Supérieure was sacked at the height of the May events, by former students and followers enraged at his continuing adherence to the PCF. Many of those responsible had been expelled from the Party in 1966 and gone on to set up various Maoist organisations. To this episode, as to the invasion of Czechoslovakia and the expulsion of Garaudy, Althusser's reponse was silence. He has been severely, and justifiably, criticised for this,[3] and the contrast with Sartre's indefatigable string of public pronouncements on one level reinforces the criticism. In another way, however, it simply shows what very different types of intellectual the two men were. To use a theological terminology appropriate to Althusser's youthful Catholic militancy, Sartre by this time was a Leftist 'worker-priest', concerned above all with the application of ideas to mass struggle, Althusser a 'pope of theory' (as he was dubbed), concerned with the rigorous development and elucidation of the fundamental concepts on which Marxism rests.

With the essay *Idéologie et appareils idéologiques d'État* [*Ideology and Ideological State Apparatuses*] of 1970, Althusser moved towards a less esoteric form of philosophy, drawing attention to the key role played in the maintenance of the bourgeois state by institutions such as the educational system and the networks of cultural production and consumption. There is no doubt that May had focused attention, in a manner quite literally unforgettable, on the importance of these 'apparatuses' in the defence of the status quo and concomitant repression of dissent. The PCF thereafter was on the horns of a dilemma, needing on the one hand to show that its attitude had been politically correct throughout and on the other to recapture the support it had lost through its hostility to the events and the movements active in them.

Althusser's essay is revelatory in this respect; Jacques Rancière (one of his collaborators on *Lire le Capital*) points out in *La Leçon d'Althusser* [*The Lesson of Althusser*] that, while clearly influenced by them, it in fact treats the events as though they had never been. *Idéologie et appareils idéologiques d'État* (known in Anglo–American academic shorthand as 'the ISAs essay') has been Althusser's most quoted piece of work in the English-speaking world, because of the importance it accords to the superstructural sphere and the relevance to film and media studies in particular of its development of the concepts of ideology and subjectivity. These aspects of the piece have tended to obscure its specific relevance to the direction the PCF was to take in the wake of 1968.

This context also illuminates Rancière's statement that Althusser 'came to sign the theoretical death-certificate of *gauchisme*'.[4] While *gauchisme* had exercised an appeal in May that went far beyond what any conventionally- organised political movement could have hoped to achieve (or itself to sustain), this was born of an inevitably short-lived conjuncture beyond which it could be predicted that the PCF would succeed in recapturing some of its lost ground. Its superior organisation and extensive working-class base helped to account for that, but another factor more important for us is the 'bank' of critical intellectuals on which it had to draw. Althusser, at the prestigious heart of the French university system, is thus described by Rancière as giving PCF intellectuals a 'prime place . . . in the concert of the university elite'.[5]

This is not to be understood as an imputation of conscious or unconscious venality to a man whose integrity is a matter of record. It can be accounted for rather by the PCF's determination to recover lost support, the high calibre of Althusser's pupils at the rue d'Ulm (which meant that they were more likely to get university posts and thus exercise influence in their turn), and the appeal to intellectuals of a rigorous theoretical approach that sought to criticise Marxist mistakes and malpractice with the finely-honed tools of Marxism itself. Rancière's jibes at the elitism of that 'Althusserianism' of which he had himself been one of the foremost beneficiaries strike an unnecessarily sour note.

Althusser's 1970s work includes two major interventions in debates within the PCF: *22ème Congrès* [*22nd Congress*], originally delivered to the Communist Students' Study Group in Paris in 1976, and *Ce qui ne peut plus durer dans le Parti Communiste* [*What can no longer go on in the Communist Party*], published initially as a series of articles in *Le Monde* in 1978. The widening scope of Althusser's interventions – from theoretical peer-group in the 1960s through to wider, educated audience – is worthy of note. *22ème Congrès* (in which May 1968 is described as 'the greatest strike in world history') warns against what Althusser saw as the rightward movement of the PCF, embodied in its abandonment of the concept of the dictatorship of the proletariat. For Althusser, to settle for socialism rather than pushing the class-struggle through to the achievement of communism is a dangerous mirage – dangerous because of the room for political manoeuvre it leaves for social democracy (a diagnosis borne out by the political evolution of many West European countries, including, arguably, France), a mirage because theoretically unsound:

> [Socialism] is an unstable period in its essence, where the class-struggle persists in 'transformed forms', unrecognisable for our own class-struggle, difficult to decipher, which can, depending on the balance of forces and the line followed, either *regress* to capitalism, *hang fire* in fixed forms, or *progress* towards communism.[6]

This develops and applies the principle, enunciated in *Réponse à John Lewis*, that there exists no socialist mode of production, and that socialism is thus an inherently contradictory type of economic organisation. One of the major theoretical points emphasised by Mao was the need to pursue the class-struggle even after the dictatorship of the proletariat had been instituted – it was in the name of this that the Cultural Revolution took place. The theoretical trap Althusser saw lying in wait for a Marxism unmindful of this basic principle was what he called in *Réponse à John Lewis* the 'economism–humanism duo', exemplified by Stalinism with its two-pronged emphasis on the rapid development of heavy industry and the cult of 'Papa Joe'.

The idea that Stalinism and humanism had anything at all in common struck many as paradoxical to say the least, and it also seemed that Althusser might be trying to have his theoretical cake and eat it; had Stalin not, after all, been hailed as a major Marxist theoretician (with admitted reservations) by Mao himself? More politically dubious still seemed to be the implication that the Gulag archipelago, the purges, and the whole apparatus of terror and repression could in some sense be traced back to a misreading of Marx. Certainly it was necessary to point out that pious condemnations of the 'cult of personality', with their implication that all that had gone wrong in the USSR over nearly thirty years could be ascribed to one supremely malevolent individual, did not constitute anything like an adequate political analysis; but Althusser's alternative appeared to overstress the importance of theoretical precision to a highly idiosyncratic extent.

The articles originally published in *Le Monde* constituted the most telling criticism of the PCF's internal practices thus far developed, if only because of the immensely prestigious source from which they came. Lack of internal democracy, compartmentalisation of discussion so that any potentially threatening moves or ideas could be isolated and neutralised, the Party leaders' obsession with scoring points off the Socialists – the criticisms were hardly new, but Althusser underscored them with a characteristic stress on the importance of theory:

> The leadership's retarded consciousness can be traced back to two causes, which in fact fuse into one: the abandonment of Marxist principles of the concrete analysis of class-relations on the one hand, and on the other the influence of bourgeois ideology on the Party, its conception of theory, and its own political practice . . . .[7]

We have reached in the Party the nadir of Marxist theory.[8]

What contribution Althusser might have been able to make to arresting the supposed decline it is impossible to say. In November 1980 he confessed to having strangled his wife, a shock given added resonance by the fact that the killing took place in his flat at the École Normale Supérieure, at the prestigious heart of French intellectual life. No charges were brought against him; he became for a long time a voluntary in-patient at the Clinique Sainte-Anne, a major centre of Lacanian psychoanalysis. Althusser had been largely responsible, through his writings and the holding for five years of Lacan's weekly seminar at the rue d'Ulm, for bringing Lacan to the attention of the French Left. The irony by which it was now a Lacanian institution that took Althusser in, however painful, is difficult to ignore.

The killing traumatised the French Left and the French intellectual world. It has been universally referred to as 'the tragedy' – by a further twist of textual irony one of the euphemisms Althusser himself used in speaking of the Stalinist era. *Le Monde* gave as full an account as possible on the following day, after which Althusser disappeared from their pages until a letter from him was published in 1984, deploring the manner in which his ideas had allegedly been misrepresented in his absence. It requires a considerable effort of self-adjustment for a British public to grasp the import of this reticence. Had a British intellectual of equivalent prominence strangled his wife, the case would undoubtedly have come to trial, nothing could have been written about it until after sentence had been passed, and headlines such as 'SHAME OF THE RED PROFESSOR' would have abounded thereafter. The privileged place of intellectuals in the French Establishment, already apparent in the failure of Sartre's repeated attempts to get himself arrested, was even more dramatically thrown into relief by the Althusser tragedy. The non-enforcement of reporting restrictions, on the other hand, makes the silence of the French press in one way difficult to understand. Garaudy, in *Le Monde*, spoke of the tragedy as an 'altruistic suicide', and of Althusser as so permeated with the idea of death that he wanted, 'in his delirium, to free those closest to him from the torment of life'. The historian (and ex-Communist) Jean Elleinstein opined that it was Althusser's theoretical reflection that so to speak pushed him over the edge. Such speculation, however, was short-lived, with the exception of an egregious piece by Edgar Morin in *Lire* of October 1981, in which he asserted without proof that Althusser 'shortly before the tragedy, had in his heart of hearts ceased believing everything he had taught, but did not dare to profess his doubt in public'.[9]

One of Althusser's most singular contributions to Marxist theory had been his insistence, in *Lire le Capital*, that *Capital*, far from being wisdom handed down on tablets of stone, was a text governed by exactly the same laws of writing as any other, and that those laws inevitably entailed significant gaps, absences, or silences in the text which it was the task of exegetes to fill out. An application of this reading to the French intellectual world's treatment of the tragedy yields interesting results. It was clear, in the period leading up to the May 1981 presidential elections, that the PCF's attempt at increasing its credibility and building its support at the expense of the Socialists had been in the long term a failure. Althusserian Marxism had come under fire for its textual fetishism, seeming indifference to history (in the name of 'anti-historicism'), and failure to make a real impact in the political (as opposed to the ideological) sphere. Within the PCF the 'Althusserians' were in a minority, as the abandonment of the dictatorship of the proletariat (a concept they had sought to maintain) clearly showed. By 1980, it was clear that Althusser represented the minority tendency within the minority party of a French Left that was generally expected to lose the coming elections. It is thus not difficult to see the vicarious suicide at which Garaudy hints as having repercussions wider than the purely personal.

Difficult, but not impossible – for the silence of the French left-wing intelligentsia in the aftermath of the tragedy can be read as an attempt to reduce it to that level. Clearly it would have been grossly insensitive to speculate too lavishly about the psychic torment of a man still alive (not that this deterred Morin), but it is questionable whether this alone motivated the silence. It was as though the tragedy amplified the growing disillusionment with Althusserian Marxism and played it back in such a way as to impede criticism of it. There can be little doubt that if it had been Althusser himself who had died then far more critical analysis of his work would have been produced. His philosophical death is figured, not only in the drying-up of his own productivity, but in the dwindling of the work that might have accounted for the political defeat of his ideas. (Ted Benton's *The Rise and Fall of Structural Marxism* is an important recent exception to this.)

Why did Althusser's work not have the political success that might have been hoped for? One major reason is certainly its ambivalent attitude towards the prospect of violent revolution. Communist parties throughout Europe moved in the seventies towards an explicitly non-revolutionary stance, exemplified by the 'historic compromise' of the Italians and the British Party's *British Road to Socialism*. This was partly an attempt to win support from socialist or social-democratic parties; partly a corresponding attempt to distance themselves from the USSR; partly the result of the theoretical influence of such writers as Gramsci or Poulantzas; and (in France at least) partly the codification of one of the major lessons of May. Paris had been ringed with tanks at the height of the events, ready to move against a possible *coup d'état*, and de Gaulle's notorious 'day-trip' to Baden-Baden to liaise with General Massu had further emphasised the possibility of bloody repression. Many on the far Left, nevertheless, exhorted the PCF to take power; its refusal to do so effectively committed it to a reformist stance thereafter, for if May had not been a 'revolutionary situation' it was difficult to see what might be. Even the overthrow of the Allende government in Chile in 1973, taken by many on the Left as clinching proof of the folly of trying to achieve socialism through the ballot-box, was absorbed into the non-revolutionary strategy, for the major lesson drawn from it by the European Communist parties was that electoral success needed to be guaranteed by the democratisation of the armed forces and other state apparatuses – both repressive and ideological, to use the distinction developed by Althusser.

The implications of Althusser's Marxism would seem to point to a belief in the inevitability of violent revolution and the consequent necessity for almost militaristic party discipline. His stress on the discontinuity of social and philosophical systems (as exemplified by his use of the 'epistemological break'); his championing of the Mao of the

Cultural Revolution; his insistence on the need to continue the class-struggle, in the form of the dictatorship of the proletariat, even under socialism – all appear to imply that talk of a peaceful transition to a socialist or communist society is a delusion, and all relate back to Althusser's most important reference-point after Marx himself, Lenin. Lenin's conception of the disciplined, democratic-centralist revolutionary organisation lay at the root of the Bolshevik Party, and has supposedly informed Communist Party organisation ever since. While Lenin himself has never been in any danger of losing his place of honour in the Marxist pantheon, increasing doubt has been cast since 1968 or thereabouts on the relevance of his ′model of party organisation to Western democratic societies, and indeed the whole 'Eurocommunist' movement can be understood as a – more or less covert – exercise in 'de-Leninisation'. Althusser's attachment to Lenin, on the other hand, remained as strong at it was unquestioned. The essay *Lénine et la philosophie* is a major attempt to establish Lenin – 'an "innocent" and an autodidact in philosophy',[10] as he is there described – as none the less a key figure in Marxist philosophical theory, and to inscribe Leninist principles into the complex theoretical domain of the relationship between ideology and science, rather than concurring with the prevalent view of Lenin as fundamentally a theorist of political organisation. Althusser's unequivocal Leninism would seem, like much else in his work, to point towards an equally unequivocal revolutionary approach, yet this is hinted at rather than boldly stated in his work. It is sweeping and unfair of Arthur Hirsch to assert (in *The French New Left*) that 'his revolutionary principles were shattered on the reefs of the PCF's electoral opportunism';[11] a more judicious formulation might be that the unceasing attempt to marry a theoretical politics predicated on rupture and discontinuity with a party-political strategy founded on the need to attract votes from as wide a range as possible was in the long run doomed to failure.

The appeal of Althusserian Marxism to intellectuals has already been suggested by the observations in Chapter 2 on the *Tel Quel* 'manifesto'. Rigour, precision, scientificity – these were qualities intellectuals were always likely to find attractive, the more so when they combined to stress the indispensable role of those same intellectuals in planning and promoting the process of social change. The relative autonomy of the ideological seemed to give intellectuals *carte blanche* to pursue their interests, without paroxysms of neo-Sartrean anxiety about whether in doing so they could be said to be 'serving the people'. The pedagogic, academic, and cultural burgeoning of Althusserian Marxism was immense, but the very factors that went to ensure this at the same time ensured that its impact in the political sphere was restricted and in the last resort comfortably countered.

This is graphically illustrated by *Sur la dictature du prolétariat* [*On the dictatorship of the proletariat*], a defence of the concept published by Althusser's pupil and collaborator Étienne Balibar in 1976, in the wake of the PCF's dropping of the concept. Balibar develops the Althusserian notion that socialism is, by definition, an unstable amalgam of contradictory forces, and that only the determined prosecution of the class-struggle can ensure the transition to communism. For both Althusser and Balibar, the dictatorship of the proletariat is the necessary condition for this, and Balibar goes so far as to denounce Stalin for declaring, in 1936, that the class-struggle in the USSR was over and that the 'State of the whole people' would thenceforth hold power. Stalin, having been denounced by Althusser in *Réponse à John Lewis* for his blend of economism and humanism, is now taken to task for prematurely terminating the dictatorship of the proletariat. The nub of Balibar's argument is that 'State power is always the power of one class. Produced in the class-struggle, State power can only be the instrument of the dominant class: what Marx and Lenin call the *dictatorship* of the dominant class'.[12] The semantic justification for the term 'dictatorship' is that 'State power cannot be divided'[13] – that, in other words, above and beyond (or, better, *before*) any legal institutions or other State apparatuses, the State is always already in the hands of one or other antagonistic class, and that the ultimate sanction for this can only be a violent one.

None of this alters the fact that the term 'dictatorship', in the France of 1976, was likely to evoke for the vast majority of people the world of Stalin and Beria rather than that of Althusser and Balibar. Althusser in *22ème congrès* ascribed the PCF's eagerness to be rid of the concept to their wish to distance themselves from Stalinism, but makes it plain that in his view this was the wrong way to go about it. 'One may "abandon" the dictatorship of the proletariat: one rediscovers it as soon as one comes to speak about the State and socialism'.[14] This is almost reminiscent of Simone Weil's 'If I appear to stray from the path that leads to Jesus in my search for truth, I will not have gone very far before I meet Him standing there' – a theology of theory that grounds itself in certain inescapable fundamentals.

However opportunistic the PCF's attitude, it seems clear with the benefit of hindsight that politically it made sense. The decline in their fortunes since 1976 is due much more to the undemocratic internal practices denounced in *Ce qui ne peut plus durer dans le parti communiste*, and to their drift back towards support for the USSR, than to the developments of the 22nd Congress. The impact of Althusser's work in the field of literary and cultural criticism, considerable as it has been, merits consideration. *Cahiers du cinéma*, under the editorship of Jean-Louis Comolli and Jean Narboni, devoted much attention from 1969 onwards to the constitution of subjectivity in cinematic texts, articulating Althusser's reading of Marx with Lacan's reading of Freud. Their analysis of John Ford's *Young Mr Lincoln* had a seminal influence on French and Anglo–American film theory and criticism. Pierre Macherey, a collaborator on *Lire le Capital*, moved in the 1970s from the Althusserian 'symptomatic readings' of *Pour une théorie de la production littéraire* [*Towards a theory of literary production*] (1966), with their stress on the necessary silences within any text and how these implictly inscribe the text's conditions of production, to a more historically-based approach. He and Balibar collaborated on the essay 'De la littérature comme forme idéologique' ['On literature as an ideological form'] – a preface to a book by Balibar's mother Renée, *Les Français fictifs* [*The Fictional French*] which explored the use of literature in the French schooling system as a means of perpetuating bourgeois ideological domination. The essay moves away from the fetishisation of the immutable text characteristic of Althusser's and Macherey's earlier work to the notion that:

the literary effect is not just produced by a determinate process, but actively inserts itself within the reproduction of other ideological effects: it is not only itself the effect of material causes, but is also an effect on socially determined individuals, constraining them materially to treat literary texts in a certain way.[15]

Figured here is an awareness of the need for close critical study and analysis of the educational system. *Idéologie et appareils idéologiques d'état* had certainly drawn attention to the system's role in helping to maintain the status quo, but Althusser scarcely went very far thereafter in suggesting how it might be worked on. Baudelot and Establet, in *L'école capitaliste en France* [*The capitalist school in France*], attempted an 'Althusserian' analysis of the national schooling system; and France Vernier, a colleague of Renée Balibar's at the (relatively) new University of Tours, devotes part of *L'écriture et les textes* [*Writing and texts*] (published by the PCF's Éditions Sociales) to a demolition of the Lagarde and Michard series of manuals which introduced generations of

French students to the 'classics' of their literature. What is interesting about Vernier's analysis is not just the targets on which she picks (the manuals' ahistorical nationalism, their unquestioning promotion of the Author of Genius as sole source of a literary work, the consequent elevation of literature to the status of a sacred mystery), but the modes of analysis she suggests. Critical dissection of secondary as well as primary sources; an awareness of the necessary contradiction in any work of literature between its roles as work of art and work of language; the need to bear in mind that literature, in Marxist terms, forms part both of the infrastructure (through its economic role and determinants) and of the superstructure (through its ideological roles) – these stem from an 'Althusserian' perspective, in their stress on the importance of contradiction and discontinuity and their insistence that these will inevitably figure the class-relations of the time at which a text was produced, but go on to take this approach into the classroom, suggesting ways in which ideology can be analysed at work in specific situations. Vernier is often a little mechanistic (as when she denounces plural readings of texts as necessarily disguising relations of class domination), but her work does indicate the pedagogical importance of developments from the work of Althusser.

Nicos Poulantzas studied under Althusser in Paris in the 1960s, and the two names are often coupled together (as at the beginning of this chapter) as 'structural Marxists'; but the political implications and impact of their work are very different. Poulantzas (along with Antonio Gramsci) was the dominant theoretical influence on the development of 'Eurocommunism', and his work on the nature of the bourgeois state and the changing class-structure of late capitalism has had an effect stretching a long way beyond the Communist movement. He came to France as an exile from the military dictatorship of the Greek colonels, and the strict French legislation barring foreigners from political activity (under which Cohn-Bendit had been refused re-entry to the country) confined his contribution to French political life largely to the domain of theory. At the same time, few other political thinkers were so responsive to the pressure of events in the 1960s and 1970s. The colonels' coup in Greece in 1967 and the May events little more than a year later between them fixed Poulantzas in that France whose philosophy (first Sartrean, then Althusserian) had exerted a major intellectual influence on him; and his work thereafter can be seen as responding to the changing fortunes of the programme of Left unity to which he meant so much and which meant so much to him.

Pouvoir politique et classes sociales [*Political power and social classes*] was Poulantzas's first major work. While Althusser had written extensively about the political sphere and its interrelationship with the economic and the ideological, there is very little consideration in his work of the manner in which societies are divided into classes, for all his insistence on the class-struggle. For Poulantzas, social classes are 'the effects . . . of certain levels of structures, including the State'[16] – the effect, in other words, of existing modes of social organisation upon the economic and political practices that take place within (or against) them. This is to say that social classes are dynamic, existing in and through the interplay of social relations and not somehow immutably prior to them (as certain conventionally ossified readings of Marx might appear to suggest). The implication of this in its turn is that, rather than merely acting to maintain at the superstructural level the economic dominance of the capitalist class, the state is what Poulantzas calls 'the structure in which are *condensed* the contradictions of the various levels of a formation . . . [and] the place which makes it possible to *decipher* the unity and the articulation of the structures of a formation'.[17] The state, in other words, is not merely an apparatus of repression. This was certainly the light in which it would have appeared to most of the French Left after the May events – the brutality of the CRS riot-police and the threat of military intervention saw to that. But, for Poulantzas, the notion of the class-struggle as a confrontation of two unchanging blocs had been overtaken and rendered obsolete by the social and economic changes of late capitalism, and it became in consequence impossible to view the state simply as a club wielded by a repressive (and potentially fascist) bourgeoisie.

To see the state as the condensation of social contradictions and antagonisms implied that it reproduced the infrastructural relations of production in bourgeois society, and thus that it actually played a part in determining these relations as well as being determined by them. This is linked with Althusser's concept of the 'relative autonomy of the three instances' (economic, political, and ideological), which while all rooted in the same social formation can develop unevenly at different periods and afford scope for specific types of local intervention depending on the conjuncture of the time. These ideas are a long way both from traditional economist Marxism and from the May events (at any rate their maximalist side), yet their effect on the one, and their connection with the other, are both evident. The explosion of May occurred at a time of apparent political and institutional stability, and, while its short-term effect for the mass of French workers was an economic one (thanks to the substantial wage-increases the major unions were able to secure), its longer-term repercussions, as we have repeatedly seen, were ideological, cultural, and to a lesser extent political. Economist Marxism simply could not account for this, nor could it provide any substantial theoretical guidelines for intervention in the cultural spheres that had been prominent in May. The ORTF broadcasting authority (broken down by Giscard in 1974 into a number of smaller bodies) had gone on strike in protest against governmental manipulation of news presentation; the Cannes Film Festival had been cancelled, and the 'Estates-General of the Cinema' met to produce proposals for major changes in the film industry; and the writers' and journalists' unions had likewise joined battle on 'superstructural' territory. Poulantzas was to go on to assert, in *L'état, le pouvoir, et le socialisme* [*State, power, and socialism*] (1978) that the base/superstructure antithesis 'has even proved disastrous in more ways than one, and there is everything to be gained from not relying on it'[18] – if not quite a rejection of this fundamental Marxist concept, then a clear indication that it was no longer indispensable.

Marx's own example (as an exile first from Germany, then from France) suggests that the experience of exile can have an effect upon the writing of political theory and analysis; *how* Marx's analysis of the societies of France and Britain would have differed if he had not been an exile in both countries (and from the first) it is difficult to say, but *that* it would have differed it is no less difficult to doubt. *Les classes sociales dals le capitalisme aujourd'hui* [*Classes in contemporary capitalism*] (1974) shows a sensitivity to the changes taking place in the European (particularly French) society of the time which it is tempting, if romantic, to ascribe to Poulantzas's status as exile, and hence perforce observer, in France. The thrust of this work is in many ways deeply critical of the 'Eurocommunist' tendency towards which the PCF was then tending. Poulantzas certainly sees the rising 'labour aristocracy' of white-collar workers and the intellectual 'technicians' of capitalism as the main part of a new *petit-bourgeoisie*, and thus as politically equivocal, much as the European Communist parties did in their attempts to win the votes of these workers at the time. But he takes the PCF to task for neglecting to pose the question of what class these groups belong to, pointing out that 'the division into class forms the frame of reference for every social stratification',[19] but at the same time that 'social formations are not in fact the concretisation and spatialization of modes of production existing already in a state of abstract purity, but rather the particular form in which the modes of production exist and are reproduced'.[20] The stress falls, in other words, at once on the necessary fact that any individual or grouping at any time belongs to one social class or another, and on the fact that such class-membership is a dynamic function of the intersection of modes and relationships of production, rather than a static, unchanging given. Poulantzas's other major criticism of the PCF here is that it fails to distinguish between the 'dominant fractions' in French society – in other words, the groupings which combine to ensure the superiority of the bourgeoisie – and the 'hegemonic fraction', by which, following Gramsci, he means the fraction that dominates the others within the dominant fractions. This division of dominant and dominated fractions, so that within each in its turn a dominant and a dominated 'sub-fraction' is to be found, recurs in the otherwise very different work of Pierre Bourdieu, which we look at in Chapter 11; it illustrates the increasing degree of subtlety required of the structural analysis of social formations in the sixties and seventies.

The PCF, according to Poulantzas, was not nearly subtle enough in *its* analysis. By oversimplifying the criss-crossing network of class determinants and positions, it effectively reduced the class-struggle in the France of the early seventies to a confrontation between 'monopoly capital' (the 'hegemonic fraction', but for Poulantzas emphatically not the only member of the class of 'dominant fractions') and the rest. Antimonopolist demonology and an often brazen courtship of partners elsewhere in the social formation certainly form a characteristic duo in the discourse of Eurocommunism, and Poulantzas's theoretical work in *Les classes sociales dans le capitalisme aujourd'hui* goes some way towards explaining why the marriage between them was neither a stable nor – in France at least – an enduring one.

The text also provides a major exegesis of Gramsci (acknowledged as an influence by Althusser, but never extensively discussed by him) and of 'the reproduction of the mental/manual labour division within mental labour itself'[21] – a hierarchisation increasingly characteristic of the French intellectual world of the time, with its 'higher' and 'lower' intelligentsia (Debray), and the structural elitism of its university system going to reinforce the historical elitism of its university personnel. Poulantzas's own place in that world was a curiously marginal one considering the importance of his work. He occupied the rank of *maître de conférences associé* at the University of Paris–VIII (Vincennes) – the equivalent grade to a British university senior lecturer (or polytechnic principal lecturer, or American university associate professor); and the suffix *associé* denotes that he did not have the kind of full academic tenure which (with very few exceptions) is granted in France only to those of French nationality. From 1976 (when he announced his break with structuralism) through to 1979 (when he explained that his original theoretical allegiance had been the result of a necessary choice between structuralism and historicism – 'Lévi-Strauss against Sartre'[22]), he moved away from the abstractionist, anti-historical tendency of his earlier work. Exile, marginality, dissatisfaction with his earlier work, disillusionment with the PCF: it is obviously impossible to ascertain how important any or all of these were in his suicide in 1979. The concluding words of *L'état, le pouvoir, et le socialisme* ('socialism will be democratic, or it will not be'[23]) suggest that the Socialist Party might have provided the most fertile ground for his work to develop. With the demise of Eurocommunism *à la française*, it is in all probability there that his work is nowadays most seriously considered.

5 Intellectuals and Marxism Since 1968 – Modes of Dissidence

So much attention has been focused on Althusserian and post-Althusserian Marxism over the last twenty or so years that one might almost conclude that it was the only significant theoretical tendency within the PCF, if not on the whole French Left. Michael Kelly's *Modern French Marxism* shows quite clearly that this is not so, and gives far more detailed accounts of other work in and around the PCF than would be possible here. One major reason for the apparent (if not real) hegemony of Althusserianism is its implantation within the intellectual and academic worlds, already noted; another is that two of Althusser's most significant theoretical opponents – each in his time regarded as the Party's leading intellectual – were expelled from the PCF: Henri Lefebvre in 1958 and Roger Garaudy in 1970.

To examine their work since 1968 is thus to ask where ex-Communists go after their break with the Party. Relatively few join other organisations (it should of course be borne in mind that the Socialist Party did not exist in its present form when Lefebvre and Garaudy were expelled); some, such as Jean Elleinstein, who contributes regularly to the extreme right-wing (and frequently anti-Semitic) *Figaro-Magazine*, move to the Right, or at least into close connection with right-wing institutions. Many, however, follow the path mapped out in very different ways by Lefebvre and Garaudy – that of non-affiliated intellectuals of the Left, exempt from the need to refer to the 'Party line', and thus developing in a manner that no doubt made them as glad to be rid of the Party's directives as the Party's leadership must have been to be rid of their incorrigible individualism.*

Lefebvre, born in 1901 (four years before Sartre), was a member of the PCF for thirty years before his expulsion. From the beginning, the basis of his adherence was, to borrow from Engels, utopian rather than scientific, for the *Philosophies* group which he helped to form in 1924 was bohemian and surrealist in its origins. (This is an interesting parallel with the early career of Jacques Lacan, in the 1930s an associate of

---

* Lefebvre has recently moved back towards a position more sympathetic to the PCF.

Georges Bataille and Jean-Louis Barrault and a regular contributor to surrealist journals.) He was expelled not only because of his public condemnations of the leadership's reluctance to de-Stalinise, but also because of the clandestine anti-Stalinist journals – as it were PCF *samizdats* – on which he had collaborated.

Lefebvre's Marxism had in its early stages been Hegelian (thus, for the leadership then and the Althusserians subsequently, 'idealistic') in its inspiration. His work after his expulsion from the Party remained characterised by the major tendency that had previously attracted criticism – an emphasis on the totality of humankind and nature, thwarted by the alienating atomisation of capitalist society. The Party had extracted from him a public self-criticism in 1948 for excessive stress on the 'neo-Hegelian' aspects of Marxist philosophy; and Althusserian Marxism, preoccupied as it was with philosophical anti-humanism and the importance of difference and contradiction, is clearly at the antipodes of Lefebvre's thought.

This in turn of course meant that Lefebvre's thought was at the antipodes of Althusser's, on which he produced some trenchant attacks throughout the sixties, collected in book form in 1971 under the title *L'idéologie structuraliste* [*The structuralist ideology*]. Much of Lefebvre's criticism rests on a discursive tactic long practised by Communist parties – the attempt to demonstrate that objectively 'left-wing' practices and arguments in fact objectively serve the interests of the bourgeoisie and of reaction. (This was, and indeed remains, the Stalinist Left's main weapon against Trotskyism.) It is the anti-historicism of structuralism – conceived of originally in opposition to the idea that human history somehow evolves inexorably towards its final goal – that is Lefebvre's principal target. He compares it at one point with the Greek philosophical school of Eleatism, which believed in the primacy of pure and immutable Being and 'dissolves mobility into segments, moments, spots, points'.[1]

Althusser's theoretical innovations, which Lefebvre discussed in two articles in 1967 and 1969, both reproduced in *L'idéologie structuraliste*, are consequently seen as 'masking, by a kind of theoretical excrescence, the absence of practical creation and of an opening onto political practice'.[2] They present, in other words, a hypertrophy of static model-making, fatally blind to the movement of history and eventually walling themselves up in a conceptual ghetto held together by its self-constitutive 'myth of rigour'.[3] For Lefebvre, such rigour is fruitless if it immobilises Marxism's founding principle, the dialectic, which if it is not kinetic is nothing. The Althusserian stress on rupture and discontinuity is disquietingly reminiscent of the very Stalinism whose (philosophical) legacy Althusser had set himself the task of (so to speak) purging; and insult is added to injury at the beginning of the later of the two articles when Lefebvre assimilates structuralist Marxism, not only to Stalinism, but to its oldest enemy – right-wing Hegelianism:

> Stalinism is a philosophical and political system. It makes present, in harsh reality, a political absolute. It places itself above philosophy, for it makes it real. Thus, for Hegel, philosophy is accomplished in and through the State: its philosophy legitimises that State of which it is the theory. Stalinism was – still is – Hegelianism in action; Stalinists were and remain right-wing Hegelians.[4]

Anglo–American readers will recognise in much of what Lefebvre says a pre-echo of E.P. Thompson's anti-structuralist diatribe in *The Poverty of Theory*. The context of the two interventions is, however, very different. Thompson was weighing-in against a development of academic Marxism that was hegemonic (for Thompson, dangerously so) on a British intellectual Left heretofore marked by solid pragmatism. Lefebvre, a prominent theoretician for almost thirty years by the time these pieces were written, would never have dreamt of entitling his essays *La pauvreté de la théorie*. His intervention – not exempt, as the last quoted passage shows, from the *'tu quoque'* tactic perfected by the Stalinists – aims at bringing theory back, through a polemical re-inscription of the very concepts Althusser most strenuously banishes, into correspondence with the political necessities of contemporary France and the rest of the world. Thus, he enters an urgent plea for the concept of alienation, however theoretically unsound Althusserians may consider it, because:

> Is the notion of alienation an operative one? Can one derive a political strategy from it? No. Is it easily detachable from the conceptual armature of Hegelianism? Hardly. Is it unambiguous, precise, analytical? No. These are the wrong questions to put. The real question is that of the role, of the practical efficacy of alienation, as an awareness of lived experience and as a concept. It brings about self-revelation for different conditions and situations (those of women, students, the colonised, the colonisers, the masters, the workers, and so on). Is it adequate to define these situations? No. And yet, for all its uncertainties, the notion is a necessary one.[5]

In the year after the May events, these remarks had a particularly persuasive ring to them. If a great many previously uncommitted people had discovered at that time new ways of looking at themselves in relation to the society in which they lived, how far was a general sense of 'alienation' an important factor in that, whatever its unsoundness from the point of view of Marxist theory? There would doubtless be those who would retort that a passing sense of disaffection is no foundation on which to build a coherent political movement, and the disparate evolution of those affected by May in the years since shows clearly that for many participants there was no more durable motivation than that. But the changed awareness discussed in Chapter 2 was undoubtedly one that affected the whole fabric of French society, and the view of the events as a spiritual crisis certainly stressed the qualitative change they wrought in many who lived through them. The Second World War and the Resistance, in a very different way, had been major formative experiences for a number of those who were to go on to be active on the Left (especially in the PCF). Beneath Lefebvre's often dubious onslaught on a preoccupation with theoretical precision that he had himself once shared, there lay an awareness of how counter-productive the jettisoning of theoretically suspect principles could turn out to be.

Althusser has asserted that, if individuals are not the subjects of history but the mere supports of economic functions, 'it is not the theoretician Marx who treats them in this way, it is capitalist relations of production'[6] – that, in other words, not Althusserian Marxism but the capitalism it denounces denies human beings their individuality. At the time Lefebvre was writing, however, Althusser had not yet moved out of the specialist-theoretical market to address himself to the condition of the workers under capitalism in quite this way, so that Lefebvre's impatience would have seemed more justified then than it may do now.

Lefebvre's impact on the movements active in May came less through his theoretical hostility to Althusser and the structuralists than through his increasing concern with 'everyday life' (a partially adequate English rendering of two French terms – *le quotidien* – which stresses the monotony of individuals' daily existence – and *le vécu*, which stresses the existential quality of their response to it). The situationist Guy Debord had been a student of Lefebvre's, and much of the 'spontaneist/ structuralist' opposition sometimes seen as a major ideological difference of May can be traced back to the conflict between the 'anti-consumerists' influenced by Lefebvre and the 'Maoists' who based their approach on a reading of Althusser. It was the politics of everyday life in its spatial and urban manifestations that Lefebvre's work in the seventies above all addressed. In an interview in December 1983 with the journal *Villes en parallèle* [*Alternative cities*], published by that same University of Nanterre where the May events had started, Lefebvre dates his interest in the political aspects of town-planning back to the establishment in 1963 of the Délégation à l'Aménagement du Territoire et à l'Action Régionale (DATAR), the governmental agency for replanning the territorial development of France. DATAR has aimed at creating more jobs in the regions, moving much economic decision-making away from Paris, and helping to co-ordinate the setting-up of new industries with the provision of environmental and infrastructural facilities. It is – in its origins at least – a technocratic phenomenon, linking that nearly two-hundred-year-old French tradition, centralised socio-economic planning, with modern technological developments and the growing realisation that the regions cannot simply be treated as milch-cows or holiday-camps for Paris. Lefebvre was the first major French thinker to see that, whatever the DATAR's limitations from a Marxist point of view, it constituted a qualitatively new type of planning, and thus a new opportunity for the Left to intervene in the politics of everyday life.

La révolution urbaine [*The urban revolution*] is his best-known work in this area. It problematises the concept of 'space', which it sees as the object alike of production and consumption, and develops the possibilities for intervention this affords. The Marxist attitude towards the city has been strongly tinged with ethical condemnation, dating back to Engels's evocation of the slums of Manchester and the nineteenth-century equation of urban development with exploitation and squalor. This is at best nowadays a debased form of neo-Rousseauism (not untinged with hypocrisy, seeing that the vast majority of left-wing intellectuals have chosen to live in such inner-city areas as Islington, Greenwich Village, or the Latin Quarter), at worst a socially destructive puritanism whose nightmarish apogee was the literal destruction of Phnom Penh by the Pol Pot regime in Cambodia. Lefebvre's ideas are in refreshing contrast; it is significant that (as he told *Villes en parallèle*), he lives in the Marais, the area of Paris most marked by redevelopment over the past ten or so years.

For Lefebvre, post-industrial society is characterised above all by being urban. The movement he traces is from an agrarian society based on need, through an industrial society based on work (and uniting its contradictory elements through the bond of surplus-value), to an urban, 'post-industrial' society based on *jouissance*. This term, prominent particularly in the work of Roland Barthes, had both a sexual sense (denoting climax), and a number of wider connotations clustering around the notion of ecstatic festivity. It was this aspect of *jouissance* that attracted Lefebvre in May, and *La révolution urbaine* makes it clear that their lesson had been an important one for him.

Space in the modern city contains and superimposes elements of all these different periods, whence the differing priorities accorded in different situations to space for work, dwelling, or culture and recreation. Lefebvre is critical of modern town-planners, not so much for blind functionalism and the pursuit of gain as for their failure to appreciate the complexity of modern urban space. For him, the town-planning of the future will need to synthesise a host of disciplines, drawing upon literature and psychoanalysis as well as sociology and economics. His continued adherence to Marxism is plain when he speaks of the contradiction between the use-value of space and its exchange-value, and, in a passage worthy of being quoted at length, of the paradox that the class whose labour made the modern city possible – the proletariat – has not yet been able to create there a space of its own:

> It is not the 'vital drive' of the urban community that explains the structures of space . . . . It is the result of a history that must be seen as the work of social 'agents' or 'labourers', or collective 'subjects', working in successive waves, producing and shaping in more or less discontinuous fashion expanses of space . . . . From their interactions, their strategies, victories and defeats, come the qualities and 'properties' of urban space. The general form of the urban brings together and envelops these multiple differences. If the Parisian example is to be believed, the proletariat has not yet created its space. The mercantile bourgeoisie, the intellectuals, the statesmen – they shaped the city. The industrialists, if anything, demolished it. As for the working class, the only space for it has been that of its expropriation and deportation: of segregation.[7]

Roger Garaudy, unique among the names discussed here in having sat as a Communist member of parliament, had, like Lefebvre, courted the disapproval of the Party's leadership for some time before his expulsion. His developing interest in Catholicism might not have mattered in the Italian Party, which has for long regarded the Church as a *frère ennemi*, but for the PCF it was cause for concern, not so much in itself as for what it revealed about Garaudy's evolution. To quote Michael Kelly, 'the speculative eclecticism of his philosophy echoed his politics of the open house from which none should be turned away'.[8] This in turn logically implied the disappearance, or at least irrelevance, of the rigorous style of organisation of which the PCF was at once the advocate and the exemplar. That Garaudy, in 1981, went on to abandon Christianity for Islam led to raised eyebrows and letters in *Le Monde*, but that too was in one way of a piece with his compulsive eclecticism; it was hardly to be expected that one who had all but advocated the disappearance of the revolutionary party would for long feel happy with the One True Church.

1968 had a twofold impact on Garaudy, who derived similar political lessons (articulated in *Le grand tournant du socialisme* [*The great socialist turning-point*]) from the May events and from the 'Prague spring'. These were spontaneist, humanist, and anti-centralist – hardly qualities likely to endear them (or him) to the Party leadership. The idea of a national strike as a major political weapon could be traced back to the anarcho-syndicalism of Georges Sorel (for a Leninist party it was a dangerously 'adventurist' concept), and that of an alliance between intellectuals and the young – students and others – to Marcuse. Garaudy's expulsion in February 1970 can have come as no great surprise to him or to his followers. *L'Alternative*, published two years after Garaudy's expulsion, is a political credo (the word is more appropriate than 'manifesto'), couched in an aphoristic, hortatory style that calls for moral as well as political renewal:

Our society is falling apart.
A fundamental transformation is needed.
It cannot come about by traditional methods.
A crisis of this scale, to be resolved, demands more than revolution: a radical qualitative change not only in the regime of property and the structures of power, but in culture and schooling, in religion and faith, in life and its meaning.
To change the world, to change life. Marx and Rimbaud.[9]

To deride this as more appropriate to a radical prelate's Easter homily than to a leading intellectual's political diagnosis would be facile, and in one sense unworthy; Marxist intellectuals since Sartre, as was earlier pointed out, have on the whole given ethical discourse a wide berth, one reason for which may be that they have fought shy of just such a reproach. Garaudy's text certainly fits in with one of the dominant trends of post-1968 left-wing thought, the rejection of economism; and his criticism of the PCF's 'anti-monopolist' stance, while much less theoretically sophisticated, is in many ways not far removed from that of Poulantzas:

An 'anti-monopolist alliance' can help to form an electoral coalition
by bringing together promises to satisfy the demands – even those
which contradict one another – of all those who have cause for
complaint against the big capitalist monopolies ... [But] the
demands of these different layers are contradictory .... An 'anti-
monopolist alliance' can thus not lead to a revolution or a qualitative
historical change, but only to a hybrid parliamentary coalition.[10]

L'Alternative also reveals an awareness of the politically fluctuating
position of intellectuals, in pointing out that 'the dominant tendency is
for a growing number of intellectuals to take part in the widespread
reproduction of capital and thereby in the creation of surplus value'[11] – in
some sort Debray *avant la lettre*. Reading the work with Garaudy's
conversion to Islam in mind, one may be struck by the stress he places on
the Third World, as ethical challenge to Western society and as possible
harbinger of its future. Garaudy speaks at one point of 'posing the
problems of the cultural revolution in the terms of our country'.[12] The
most successful cultural revolution of recent times, as Debray was not
slow to assert, was that carried out in the name of Shi'ite Islam by the
Ayatollah Khomeini in Iran – that same Ayatollah to whom Garaudy
claims the West owes 'an immense debt.'[13] The irony of Garaudy's
conversion is perhaps that his eclecticism finally stretched to encompass
a movement which in its most visible and politically pertinent mani-
festation at least must count among the least eclectic the modern world
has seen.

6 The Politics of Psychoanalysis

The greatest single change in the French intellectual landscape since the beginning of the 1960s is the vastly increased prominence of psychoanalysis. That may appear to be a doubly contestable statement. On the one hand, Jacques Lacan, the dominant figure in the area, had been developing his theories ever since the publication of his thesis in 1932; on the other, other tendencies, notably feminism and antipsychiatry, can be said to vie with psychoanalysis for theoretical prominence. But the radical shift in the status of psychoanalysis, from marginal intruder upon French culture to intellectually – and often also existentially – hegemonic force, cannot be adequately understood unless one takes into account the equally radical shift towards a political re-evaluation of the self, and a self-based re-evaluation of the political, epitomised by the May events. Feminism and antipsychiatry (certainly in their French manifestations) owe a great deal to Lacanian theory, even at their points of most acrimonious divergence from it. Lacan can indeed be said to be the most seminal (the pun is intended, and will be justified) French thinker of our period, for not only feminism and antipsychiatry but also structuralist Marxism, Foucault's re-examination of history and power, and the literary deconstruction of such as Derrida and Lyotard would not be what they are and have been without his contribution.

That is true, not only of the substantive content of the movements in question, but of the climate in which they grew and prospered. One rather unfortunate result of the recent anti-historicist tendencies in French intellectual life has been that theories, schemas, and models have often been discussed in abstract, quasi-theological terms of 'truth' and 'falsehood', and the no less well-trodden pathway from intellectual divergence to personal obloquy – well-trodden at least since the Sartre/Camus quarrel – has been made a great deal easier by the muting or occluding of the mediating discourses of historical and social change. A good example of this, to be taken up in Chapter 11, is Pierre Bourdieu's critique, in the final section of *La Distinction*, of what he sees as Derrida's philosophical aestheticism. Considerable bad feeling apparently arose between the two men – fellow *khâgneux* and *normaliens* – because of Bourdieu's contention that philosophy, even at its most radically deconstructive, remains grounded in an implicit aesthetics of taste. What is of interest here is the difficulty – the scandal even – presented by any such attempt to relativise and contextualise, through a stress on the particular institutional determinants of philosophy in France, a conceptual stance. The inconsistency between on the one hand theoretical positions which perceive all textuality as relative and context-bound (Derrida); all sexuality as socially constructed and incorporating the exercise of power (Foucault); or the 'Holy Writ' of Marx itself as subject to the same laws of silence and absence as any other text (Althusser); and, on the other, the fervently canonical mode in which such positions tend to be articulated and defended – between the socially and historically determined content of the ideas and their often para-theological form – is one of the most striking features of modern French intellectual life. So lengthy a caveat is nowhere more necessary than in any attempt to address not only Lacan, but also his impact. His nonpareil self-presentation as *monstre sacré* of two establishments (that of psychoanalysis and that of the Left Bank intelligentsia); the tactical deployment of textuality throughout his work to tyrannise as well as to stimulate; the venom of his onslaughts on opponents or (worse still) ex-disciples: these are all sufficiently well-documented not to need extensive presentation here. The ambiguity of his relationship with the Catholic Church contributes interestingly to the view of Lacan as a Dostoevskyan 'Grand Inquisitor' of psychoanalysis. His brother (to whom Lacan's doctoral thesis is dedicated) is a prominent Jesuit theologian; one major attack on his arrogance and intolerance featured the papal keys emblematically on the front cover; it has been rumoured that he delayed marrying his wife (the film actress Sylvia Bataille) until her first husband, the philsopher Georges Bataille, was dead, out of respect for Church teaching on the indissolubility of marriage. Whether or not this is true, the significant thing is that such a rumour was perceived as credible. A frequent Lacanian mode of addressing selected collaborators was with the Biblical pun 'You are Peter, and upon this rock I will build my Church' (the play on words is far more effective in French because both 'Peter' and 'rock' are rendered by '*pierre*').[1] Plays on words occupy an important place in Catholic theology (the notorious Jesuitical sophistry is in one sense but the most developed version of them), and the sense of atemporal mastery they seem to confer on the 'punster' or aphorist – the impression that one is present at a reversal of the normal order of linguistic temporality, where rather than being the bearer and subject of language as in 'everyday' speech the individual detaches him/herself from language and performatively asserts mastery over it – was one that Lacan assiduously, and successfully, cultivated.

As well as being at least as much a 'pope of theory' as Althusser, Lacan, with commendable ecumenism, contrived to appear at the same time as the most guru-like of French thinkers. Anglo–American culture in our period was far more affected than its French counterpart by (often commercialised) aspects of Oriental culture: music, mysticism, and religion. The more politicised French view of the Orient (notably of course China), and the strong anti-mystical streak which has long imbued French non-Catholic culture, help to account for this. If there was an Oriental 'guru-figure' in France in the late sixties, it was not the Maharishi Mashesh Yogi, but Mao Zedong. This is relevant to an understanding of the context in which Lacan operated because a great many of his most fervent disciples came originally from wealthy Catholic families and later found their way to the Lacanian seminar and the psychoanalyst's couch by way of the 'detour' through Maoist politics. Thus it was that René Lourau, in *Le lapsus des intellectuels*, was able to speak of the overlap between '*le culte du Mao*' and '*le culte du moâ*' (the pun here is that '*moâ*' transliterates an 'upper-class' pronunciation of '*moi*', thus hinting at the likely social origins of those involved).[2]

This is not to say that psychoanalysis necessarily represented an alternative to political militancy; for Althusser, as we have seen, the two were conjugated in such a way as to illuminate and reinforce each other, and the watertight division between 'personal' and 'political' could no longer be maintained after the experiences of May and the women's movement. But the fact remains that a great many of those disappointed by the seeming ephemerality of the May events, and later by the 1970s electoral failures of the Left, came to find in psychoanalysis the best available channel for the critical energies of which they had become conscious. It would be hard to overestimate the role played in this by Lacan's carefully-constructed persona – a guru to succeed Mao, but also a patriarch in opposition to the paternalism rooted in French society and symbolised above all by de Gaulle. The thrust of Lacan's theories, in this respect, is profoundly ambiguous. They draw unceasing attention to the role of the father as law-maker, censor, and ultimately castrating tyrant (the '*nom du Père*', or 'name of the Father' – which for Lacan represents the child's entry into the differential world of language – is also the '*non du Père*', the father's 'no' or refusal, initially but not solely to the son's sexual desire for the mother). They also seek to undermine the determinate role of biology, by substituting for the penis which is for

Freud the object of female desire the concept of the phallus – not a biological organ, but a nexus of relations linked at once with sexuality and with power. Sherry Turkle, whose *Psychoanalytic Politics* is an excellent introduction to Lacan's thought in its specifically French context (this chapter owes much to it), distils this well when she says:

> In Lacan's work, the phallus does not stand for the penis itself. It stands for the infant's absolute and irreducible desire to be a part of the mother, to be what she most desires. We shall see that for Lacan it comes to stand, even more generally, for the kind of desire that can never be satisfied.[3]

Stress on the tyranny of paternalism, on language as ideological and libidinal battleground, on the necessary insatiability of desire rather than on its supposed fixation on a biological organ: these clearly subvert the implicit presuppositions on which bourgeois society and its politics of the family rest, and it is not difficult to see why in the wake of 1968 their attraction was such a powerful one. Lacan's flamboyant anti-Americanism dovetailed interestingly with this; it was based largely upon his scorn for American ego-psychology as a form of social engineering, whose aim is to bring the malfunctioning individual back into smooth synchrony with the society of which s/he is part. For Lacan, this was doubly pernicious nonsense, resting at it did upon a naïve faith in the autonomous ego and upon a view of the social order as a machine for the production of happiness which merely required the periodic oiling of some of its more recalcitrant parts. Since the Lacanian problematic denies the autonomy of the ego (which it views as the source of illness and neurosis rather than of strength and resolve), and considers the social order as a tissue of linguistic and phenomenal contradictions rather than as a smoothly-functioning whole, it is hardly surprising that his distance from the Americanisation of Freud should be so considerable and so vociferous.

The political implications of this, however, are highly ambiguous. From the elitist sociology of de Tocqueville through to the foreign policy of de Gaulle, anti-Americanism has never been the sole preserve of the Left in France, and Lacan's stress on the ways in which desire is condemned to non-fulfilment can be read as destructive of any political project, pointing rather towards the metaphysical nihilism that informs the work of the 'new philosophers' or the social nihilism that informs that of Jean Baudrillard. His theoretical development of the links between sexuality, power, and language, whose importance it is practically impossible to overestimate, also has its share of political ambiguities. Many of these stem from the histrionic quality of his public performances, which as well as being elaborations of theory were also theatrical exercises in the deployment of his own unconscious. The coerciveness of his style, which went hand-in-hand with an often-expressed contempt for his audience, even led to allegations of theoretical 'fascism' in certain quarters, and his notorious tendency to give analytical sessions of five or ten minutes at colossal expense reinforced the tendency of many to think of him as a nakedly opportunistic charlatan – Diderot's Rameau's Nephew without the disarming honesty and augmented by the full panoply of the academic and media worlds.

Lacan's own biography – a highly constructed narrative if ever there was one – reinforces the view of him, for good or for ill, as a *monstre sacré*. Scissions, expulsions, and excommunications constantly beset the various psychoanalytic institutions with which he was involved, from his first exclusion from the International Psychoanalytic Association in 1953 through to his discussion of his own École Freudienne de Paris in 1980. So radical a re-reading and re-inscription of the work of Freud was bound to provoke dissent, and it is no part of this study to apportion the 'rights' and 'wrongs' of the various disputes. It would be more fruitful to pursue the implications of Derrida's observation that 'the new status for us to discover is that of the relationship between life and text, between these two forms of textuality and the general writing in the play of which they are inscribed'.[4] What this means, summarily, is that to treat the body of work and the biological and biographical body that produced it as though they were totally unconnected is as limiting an approach as the old biographical school of criticism, in which texts were valuable for what they told us about their author and vice versa. Particularly when dealing with a thinker such as Lacan, whose biography, as narrative and as theatre, is so difficult to separate from his writings, the approach suggested by Derrida comes close to being the only satisfactory one. In the 'two forms of textuality' that are Lacan-the-man and 'Lacan'-the-work, scission, separation, and literally traumatic contradiction are important features, and the influence of his work on contemporary French intellectual life has been so immense that it is not surprising that – as by a kind of textual contagion – these features have seemed almost to dominate it in the period under consideration.

They had made an important appearance at another time of socio-political crisis – the period between the wars – with the surrealists, Lacan's early associates. The similarities between aspects of the May events and surrealism have already been noted, and the distinctive contribution of Lacan was among other things to appear to bring together the theatrical eccentricities of the surrealists with a rigorous science of the unconscious analogous (for Althusser, in *Freud et Lacan*) to Marx's science of history. Again, it was the promise of liberation and scientificity combined that exercised so potent a seduction, though this combination was in many respects to prove as unrealisable theoretically as it was politically.

Lacan's own interest in politics could most charitably be described as erratic. He maintained relations with Althusser, who was responsible for hosting his seminar at the rue d'Ulm; he was a strong supporter of the student movement in 1968, whether out of nostalgia for his own surrealist youth or of a presentiment that many of the energies unleashed might one day find their way (back) to him, in accordance with his own stress on *ce qui revient au Père* (that which – always – comes back to the father); the emphasis he placed throughout his work on the non-transparency of language constituted a devastating theoretical demolition of the Gaullist and post-Gaullist insistence on 'dialogue' and 'participation' as the keynotes of a would-be humanised capitalism. But it is difficult to read these disparate phenomena along with the autocracy of his style in such a way as to produce any kind of coherent political position, expressed or implied; and this is clearly figured in the divergent paths taken by many of his followers.

A political stance in contemporary Paris, however, is not – cannot be – simply the sum of attitudes and pronouncements. The institutional dimension is also extremely important, and in this respect Lacan's relations with the University of Vincennes (Paris–VIII) merit some attention. Well before 1968, he had scandalised the French psycho-analytic establishment by his introduction of the principle of self-authorisation in the École Freudienne de Paris. Sherry Turkle points out that 'the idea of self-authorisation directly challenges what is for most the reassuring notion that psychoanalysis, like other professions, and particularly like other medical specialities, works with a close standard of quality control',[5] and her account of the procedure of the 'pass', in which analysands within the school vetted prospective analysts, under the close personal control of Lacan, illustrates the ambiguity of this approach.[6] Thus, when invited to help to set up a department of psycho-analysis at Vincennes, Lacan was responsible for appointing a number of staff who were not 'properly' qualified analysts, notably his son-in-law, Jacques-Alain Miller, a philosopher by training. The department gave credits to everybody who enrolled for a course (a compromise between the students' desire to have their work rewarded and the staff's insistence on a position of subversive marginality), and propagated a hagiographic attitude towards *Le Maître* that had bizarre intellectual and personal results. Lacan himself delivered one lecture there (in December 1969), which was rowdily interrupted and in the middle of which one student stripped half-naked. Lacan responded by berating the students as clowns of the most inane kind, playing into the hands of the regime, and by assuring them that, since they wanted a master, that was what they would undoubtedly get. Of the accuracy of that remark there is little doubt; the subsequent demolition of Vincennes alone saw to that. Less than five years after his lecture, however, Lacan appeared to have forgiven – or condemned? – the institution sufficiently to name himself scientific director of a totally revamped department, henceforth known as '*le champ freudien*' ('the Freudian field'). The tension between personal and psychic liberation and scientific knowledge had found in the Vincennes department of psychoanalysis its most dramatic institutional focus.

A moderately attentive reading of Lacan will show that such a tension, for him, is not in fact a major issue. His distaste for the libertarian Anglo–American schools of anti-psychiatry (R. D. Laing, David Cooper, Thomas Szasz) is well documented, and the whole thrust of his work is towards the inexorability of the Letter and the Law, set forth as much in the philosophical dialectic of Hegel or the word-games of Joyce and the surrealists as in the work of Lévi-Strauss or of Freud himself. Schematically, it is possible to say that Lacan and Althusser (two names often coupled together, in a variety of contexts) have in common that, while much of their appeal contextually at least was to the desire for liberation from existing structures and patterns of thought, the claims to scientificity that pervade their work made such a liberation at best a provisional one – for as long, that is, as one remained loyal to them. The mixture of continued admiration for and interest in their work with the desire to go beyond it that informs many of the writers considered later in this study doubtless stems from this contradiction, among other things. Catherine Clément, cultural editor of the socialist daily *Le Matin de Paris*, and one of Lacan's most fervent admirers, delivers a caustic denunciation of many erstwhile 'Althussero–Lacanians' in her *Vies et légendes de Jacques Lacan* [*Lives and legends of Jacques Lacan*]:

History is crafty, that we know. One of its most cunning tricks was to attach to Lacan and Althusser a bunch of kids whose pathway through life often leads them to deny those close to them. The little philosophers at the École Normale, who followed at the same time and with the same enthusiasm the teachings of 'new-wave' Marxism and those of trendy psychoanalysis, became, as we know, ardent Maoist militants towards the end of the 68 movement. That was not illogical. But it is certain that the twofold lessons had been heard in a very funny way. From Althusser, or from his unconscious, the young philosophers heard the need to found a communist movement unlike the Soviet model, and thus unlike the current French model – despite the presence of a General Secretary, Waldeck-Rochet, who was of a very different kind, in style and in thought, from the current leaders of the PCF. China was quite a good representation of this new model – the more so as it was little known, so that one could project upon it, exotically, all the theoretical fantasies one wished. From Lacan's teachings, the children of Althusser heard the pitiless determinism of the unconscious, and the illusoriness of freedom. This amounted to a belief that one could replace the imaginary by a suitable kind of pedagogy, and by a 'cultural revolution' whose dogmatism set sensitive souls on fire, precisely because it wrung the neck of a clear conscience. But, here again, the unconscious had done its work well: for Lacan was indeed in search of a pedagogy, and a morality stemming from it.[7]

This text has been quoted at length not so much for its splenetic tone as for the way in which it brings together many of the dramatis personae – individuals, institutions, cultural and contextual factors – that have occupied us thus far. The 'new philosophers', the 'post-structuralists' such as Derrida and Lyotard, other thinkers (such as Baudrillard) sceptical about or hostile to Marxism as to any supposedly referential system – all these writers and currents can be better understood in the context Catherine Clément here evokes, a context whose dominating figure (if only because he never underwent a clear political defeat) appears more and more clearly now to be that of Lacan.

7 The Politics of Feminism

The point, emphasised in the previous chapter, that Lacan's concept of the phallus marks a shift away from the biological determination of subjectivity and sexuality requires important qualification – has, indeed, received just that, notably from feminists critical of the phallocracy of his practice. One of his seminars was devoted to the question posed by Freud in a letter to Marie Bonaparte ('The great question that has never been answered and which I have never yet been able to answer, despite my thirty years of research into the feminine soul, is "What does a woman want?"'). Lacan's answer to (or gloss on) the Freudian enigma includes the following:

> just as with Saint Teresa – you only have to go and look at the Bernini statue in Rome to understand immediately she's coming, no doubt about it. And what is she enjoying, coming from? It's clear that the essential testimony of the mystics is that of saying they experience it but know nothing about it . . . I believe in the *jouissance* of the woman in so far as it is *en plus*, something more, on condition you block out that *more* until I've thoroughly explained it.[1]

Stephen Heath, in the important article from which the above two quotations are taken, says of Lacan's seminar that

> any answer to the questions posed will be in terms of the identification of a discourse that is finally masculine, not because of some conception of theory as male but because in the last resort any discourse which fails to take account of the problem of sexual difference in its enunciation and address will be, within a patriarchal order, precisely indifferent, a reflection of male domination.[2]

The specific kind of 'male domination' in Lacan's comments can be said to reside in their robustly self-evident quality and their willingness to accept feminine specificity and autonomy *if* Lacan himself holds exclusive rights to explain these. Heath goes on to point out that the primacy Lacan's discourse unquestioningly accords to seeing will inevitably strengthen the biological prominence, as it were, of the male genitals, and thus undercut the claim that the Lacanian phallus represents an escape from the tyranny of the biological.

That tyranny became evident in the biographical as well as theoretical text in 1974, when, immediately after Lacan's effective *coup d'état* at Vincennes, Luce Irigaray (who taught there and was a member of the École Freudienne) wished to start a course based on her new book, *Speculum ou l'autre femme* [*Speculum or the other woman*]. Lacan's peremptory rejection of this proposal aroused a great deal of hostility, not merely as another example of how impossible he was but as evidence of his overweening phallocracy. There would seem to be no area of Western discourse over which he did not at least implicitly stake out territorial rights, and when one such area was that inhabited by a majority of the population that did not include him, severe criticism was the least that might have been expected to result.

In order to understand more fully the import and context of this, we need to go back to 1970 and the foundation of the French women's liberation movement (MLF). May had focused attention among other things on the benighted and oppressive attitudes towards women in French society, but all too often by way of an 'alternative' attitude no less benighted and oppressive. Boasting about sexual exploits on the barricades formed an important part of the swiftly-generated mythology of 1968 (there is a clear parallel here with the British and American 'permissive societies' of the time), and the gay activist and writer Guy Hocquenghem declared caustically in the tenth-anniversary issue of *Autrement* that 'May ... gave his final blaze of glory to the guy-in-battle-dress-whose-woman-puts-on-the-coffee',[3] pointing out at the same time that notices put up by a gay group had been summarily torn down in May. If the May events marked in a real sense the end of anything at all, it was of the unquestioned prevalence of a view of male sexuality very little different from that of the lascivious scion of the well-off climbing into the family car on a Saturday night to lose his virginity for the first, or fiftieth, time.

The emergence of gay and feminist movements in the early seventies is one of the most important developments of the period since 1968 (Front Homosexuel d'Action Révolutionnaire [FHAR], in 1971; *Choisir*, demanding an end to the legal ban on abortion, in 1972), but well enough documented elsewhere not to require detailed treatment here. Despite the swingeing Catholic condemnations of homosexuality, French writers and intellectuals in the twentieth century at least had very little compunction about 'coming out'; the examples of Cocteau (who became a highly unorthodox Catholic while remaining a practising homosexual) and Gide (an atheist of Protestant origin, much of whose life and work was a sustained plea for the superiority, rather than the mere acceptability, of homosexual love) readily spring to mind. Foucault and Barthes, the latter of whom acknowledged the influence of the by-then unfashionable Gide on his work, continued this trend into our period.

The French intellectual climate, even on the Left, has thus on the whole been more unfavourable to women (whatever their sexuality) than to homosexual men. This had much to do with the climate of Catholic advocacy of obligatory female fertility, and (until 1975) the consequent ban on abortion. One major influence on the lifting of this was the *Manifeste des 343 'salopes'* of 1971. This was a public statement, signed by 343 women of varying degrees of prominence, saying that they had had abortions and felt that every woman should have the right to choose one. The word '*salope*' (= slut, bitch) is here a projective term of male abuse for a female who exercises her sexual freedom (which of course includes the freedom to reject); its use here was thus a doubly shocking one, since on the one hand women were actually laying claim to what had been intended as an insulting label and on the other those women included such as the feminist lawyer Gisèle Halimi, the actresses Catherine Deneuve and Delphine Seyrig, and Simone de Beauvoir – hardly the kind of people the average French male would think of as '*salopes*'. Much feminist effort in the earlier part of our period went into the abortion campaign. It was at the height of this – what might be called the 'first wave' of modern French feminism – that de Beauvoir declared, in a *Nouvel Observateur* interview: 'I am a feminist today because I realised that we must fight for the situation of women, here and now, before our dreams of socialism can come true'.[4] Hitherto de Beauvoir's attitude (which was also the dominant one on the orthodox Left) had been that the struggle for socialism included and subsumed the struggle for women's emancipation, that the liberation of parts of humanity would come through the liberation of the whole. Expressed in that way, the position appears absurd, yet it was widely, if implicitly, accepted.

It is interesting in this connection to look at the interview between de Beauvoir and Sartre in *L'Arc*, in which the following passage appears:

[*de Beauvoir*]: I have to say that you have never oppressed me, and that you have never shown any sense of superiority towards me. To tone down your machismo, it is important to see that we have never had a relationship of inferiority/superiority, as often happens between a woman and a man.

[*Sartre*]: In this very relationship, I learned to understand that there were kinds of relationship between man and woman which pointed to the basic equality of the two sexes. I did not consider myself superior to you, or more intelligent, or more active, so I put us on the same level. We were equals. I think, oddly enough, that that reinforced my machismo in a way, because it made it possible for me, when I was with other women, to become a macho again. Yet our equality did not simply seem to me to be a de facto equality between two individuals, but a revelation of the basic equality of the two sexes.[5]

The qualities of what had been, for a great many people in France and elsewhere, the very paradigm of an emancipated male/female relationship come through vividly in this extract. As intellectuals constantly, and through a conscious act of choice, in the public eye, it was inevitable that de Beauvoir and Sartre should see the significance of their relationship as going beyond the two of them; yet it is equally significant that it was Sartre (admittedly in this context the 'interviewee') who moved the ground of the discussion from the particular to the general, from the interplay between two individuals to a representation of all that male/female relationships could be and might become.

There is, however, little doubt that the emergence of the women's movement, and de Beauvoir's proclamation of adherence to it, helped her to emerge from Sartre's shadow in the seventies. She formed a link between the 'old' emancipation and the 'new' feminism whose importance is difficult to overestimate, as is shown in her seventieth-birthday interview with Alice Schwarzer in 1978:

There's something else I would very much like to do if I were thirty or forty now, and that is a work on psychoanalysis. I would not take Freud as my starting-point, but go right back to basics and from a feminist perspective, from a feminine rather than a masculine stand-point. But I shan't do it. I don't have enough time ahead of me. Other women will have to do it.[6]

Sartre had a long-standing interest in Freud (he wrote the screenplay for John Huston's film *Freud, or the secret passion*, of 1962), but his commitment to the conception of human freedom and existential choice would seem to have little common ground with the Lacanian version of psychoanalysis. Yet there are striking similarities of vocabulary, such as the importance both attach to the gaze or look (*le regard*) as simultaneously constitutive and threatening, and even more perhaps the stress on the Other (*l'Autre*) as a major psychic determinant, whether through presence or absence. This may suggest one of the ways in which the existentialism of de Beauvoir's work was able to find some common ground with post-Lacanian and other modern theoretical developments. This is illustrated by the number of *L'Arc* already quoted – *Simone de Beauvoir et la lutte des femmes* [*Simone de Beauvoir and the women's struggle*], which along with the Sartre interview includes work by the 'latter-day' feminist writers Hélène Cixous, Catherine Clément, and Christine Delphy – and by de Beauvoir's founding editorship of *Questions féminines*, a radical feminist theoretical journal, in 1977. De Beauvoir may have begun the seventies by being attacked in a feminist journal (*L'an zéro*) for her 'fixation' on Sartre, but she ended the decade (and not for reasons of age or health alone) more in tune with, and influential upon, contemporary French intellectual developments than the man whose 'disciple' she was so often called.

It was, moreover, in *Les Temps Modernes* that feminist ideas and themes made one of their most important moves from a restricted to a more general market. The special 1974 issue (*Les femmes s'entêtent* – a threefold pun on 'women without a head', hundred-headed women', and 'women becoming stubborn') was perhaps less important in the long run than the regular section devoted to 'le sexisme ordinaire' ('everyday sexism'), which has been running now for eleven years. It was in *Les Temps Modernes*, in 1978, that there appeared one of the most vehement attacks on Lacan and his methods, by Dominique Maugendre. The thrust of the criticism was twofold, directed against the alleged dressing-up of pell-mell eclecticism as theory and against Lacan's own domineering methods:

> [Lacan's theory is] a very heterogeneous mixture whose principal components are: philosophy transformed in its totality by the discovery of the unconscious, a dash of Saussurean linguistics, a pinch of structuralism, a few drops of Marxism, Freudianism in its entirety, mathematics, and a smattering of physiology, biochemistry, medicine, ethnology, and so forth . . . The essential difference between this Theory and theory is that one man, and one man alone, holds the secret of the right balance of ingredients.[7]

This bears some resemblance to the disabused remarks of Denis

Kambouchner in *Autrement* at almost exactly the same time,[8] but the major difference is that Maugendre's is quite literally an *argumentum ad hominem*, directed against Lacan's phallocracy as well as his authoritarianism. Francis George, a member of the editorial board of *Les Temps Modernes*, published an anti-Lacanian pamphlet (*Lacan ou l'effet yau de poêle*), extracts from which were reproduced in the journal in 1979. The title alludes to a French pun (*'Comment vas-tu?'* - 'How are you?' being responded to with *'yau de poêle'*, *'tuyau de poêle'* meaning 'stovepipe'), which like much English 'end-of-the pier' humour is meant to produce laughter through its monumental unfunniness, and George aims not only at criticising Lacan, but at deflating the pretended significance of his work, and its reliance on word-play. This he dismisses as 'spoonerisms rejected by *Le Canard Enchaîné* [a French satirical magazine]',[9] and Lacan himself is assimilated (by a process one suspects he might well not have disavowed) to Lewis Carroll's Humpty Dumpty, who used words to mean whatever he wanted them to mean. The most severe criticism, reinforcing that of Dominique Maugendre, is that 'Lacanian teaching is not the transmission of knowledge, but the exercise of mastery'.[10] It is interesting to note the role played by *Les Temps Modernes* in the late seventies in producing and diffusing criticism of Lacan.

It is, however, the women's movement which has provided the most sustained theoretical development from, and critique of, psychoanalysis. Many French feminists were strongly hostile to Freud, who was seen as supplying patriarchy with its ultimate rationalisation; but many conversely were sectarian in their adherence to psychoanalytic theory. This was particularly true of the group 'psychanalyse et politique', which became known in its subsequent avatar, when it controlled the publishing-house Éditions des Femmes, as *'psy at po'*. Its best-known mouthpiece was Antoinette Fouqué, generally known simply as 'Antoinette'. A 1973 interview with *Le Nouvel Observateur* conveys the rigorously apodictic fervour of this grouping:

> If capitalism is based on the sexual division of work, the women's struggle is based on sexual difference. The only discourse on sexuality that exists is the psychoanalytic discourse. Therefore the women's struggle must of necessity deal with the dialectical relationship between historical materialism and psychoanalysis.[11]

In fairness to Antoinette, it should be pointed out that her reference to psychoanalysis as 'the only discourse on sexuality that exists' does not deny the existence of (for example) the sixth commandment; the term 'sexuality' is here to be understood in a very specific way, relating to the (symbolic and scientific) articulation of sexual difference that psychoanalysis – perhaps since Freud, certainly in its post-Lacanian manifestations – has taken as its object.

Nevertheless, 'psy et po' was found far too coercive by a great many women (and others), whether themselves psychoanalysts or not. A more suggestive and culturally open approach to the conjunction of (Freudian) psychoanalysis and (Marxist) historical materialism was found in the work of Julia Kristeva. This is considered in Chapter 9 rather than here because its main context has been the 'politics of language' variously explored by Barthes, Derrida, and *Tel Quel*, rather than (though not excluding) the specifically feminist writers dealt with in this chapter.

Prominent among these is Luce Irigaray, whose shabby treatment by Lacan has already been mentioned. The title of her second major work, *Ce sexe qui n'en est pas un* [*This sex which is not one*], is a punning epigraph for her attempt to counterpose a writing of the female body to the traditional male sense of phallic dominance and superiority. 'This sex' is *not* one in so far as it is denied by male (especially Freudian) discourse, but also not *one* in its plurality of focuses and erogeneous zones. Irigaray does not understand by this merely zones that can respond to the stimulation of a partner (of either sex), for she is equally concerned with woman's supposedly richer capacity for self-stimulation:

He [man] needs an instrument in order to touch himself: his hand, women's genitals, language. And this self-stimulation requires a minimum of activity. But a woman touches herself by and within herself directly without mediation, and before any distinction between activity and passivity is possible. A woman 'touches herself' constantly without anyone being able to forbid her to do so, for her sex is composed of two lips which embrace continually. Thus, within herself she is already two – but not divisible into ones – who stimulate each other.[12]

In order to understand how Irigaray is able to derive from this vision of the female body her view of what a specifically female language and relationship to the unconscious might be, we need to be aware of the tissue of punning relationships that links the French words *corps* (body) and *texte* (text). It is common to speak, in both English and French, of a 'body of texts', yet the interrelationship between the two words is often thereby passed over. We tend to assimilate the constructed artefact that is a (literary or other) text to the organic system that is a 'body', and much structuralist and post-structuralist criticism, notably that of Roland Barthes, draws extensively on this.

Thus it is that in *Le plaisir du texte* [*The pleasure of the text*] Barthes is able to speak of *jouissance*, which refers originally to sexual climax, in a literary and thus textual sense. The converse of this is that the biological body, for psychoanalysis, can be treated as a 'text' – in the obvious sense that it can be 'read' and deciphered, as with psychosomatic symptoms, but also in that it exists for the psyche as an assembly or weaving-together (and the word 'text' derives from the Latin word for 'to weave') of discrete parts.

The physical body, in other words, is no more a simple given than the written text of whose nature it partakes (and vice versa). Barthes, Lacan, and Derrida all draw extensively on this major current in modern French thought, which also contextually illuminates Althusser's preoccupation with the relationship between Marxist 'text' and the 'body' of society. For Irigaray, the specificity of the texts women produce – of the feminine use of language – is rooted in the specificity of their relationship to their own bodies. This is figured in the final section of *Ce sexe qui n'en est pas un*, 'Quand nos lèvres se parlent' ['When our lips speak to each other'], where she says:

If we [women] do not invent a language, if we do not find its language, our body will have too few gestures to accompany our history. We shall be tired of the same ones, which leave our desire latent and waiting. We shall go back to sleep, dissatisfied. And handed over to the words of men. Who have known for a long time. But *not our body*.[13]

Irigaray's approach comes close to being a 'reverse biologism', counter-posing to the centuries of male assertion of superiority because of the visibility of the penis what might be called a feminist *nos quoque*. This is not (or not solely) an affronted male squeal of revulsion at a taste – or the taste – of one's own sex's medicine; what is here questioned (and has been questioned too by female readers of Irigaray) is the primacy at least implicitly accorded to the body as physical and biological given, as a sexed condition from which there is no escape and which must inevitably reinscribe itself in a similar way at every level of activity. The poly-morphousness of male desire (more prevalent, or at least more widely acknowledged, perhaps among homosexual men) and the non-normativeness of female desire both seem underrated by much that Irigaray says. The fact that the address of *Ce sexe qui n'en est pas un* is implicitly to a female readership, yet that males can 'understand' the work from a position that is not simply one of voyeuristic spectatorship, itself undercuts and deconstructs the binary sexual opposition on which the book appears to rest.

Another writer who has worked extensively on the specificity of women's writing, from within yet also against a theoretical psychoanalytic perspective, is Hélène Cixous. Her most celebrated text is *Le rire de la Méduse* [*The laughter of the Medusa*], which takes up the Greek mythical archetype of the petrifying or immobilising woman that had fascinated the writer Michel Leiris among others. *Le rire de la Méduse* stresses women's potential for a global (not to say cosmic) disruption of the existing social, economic, and textual order. This may seem to sit incongruously with more 'traditional' feminist views of women's exploitation and marginality, but for Cixous it is precisely their exclusion from male schemes of classification and partition that gives women such potential in so wide an area. Thus:

A feminine text cannot fail to be more than subversive. It is volcanic; as it is written it brings about an upheaval of the old property crust, carrier of masculine investments; there's no other way. There's no room for her if she's not a he. If she's a her-she, it's in order to smash everything, to shatter the framework of institutions, to blow up the law, to break up the 'truth' with laughter . . . If there is a 'propriety of woman', it is paradoxically her capacity to depropriate unselfishly, body without end, without appendage, without principal 'parts'.[14]

Cixous's own work – as university teacher of literature, theoretician, essayist, and (to use a conveniently loose term) 'creative writer' – figures the 'depropriation', the sweeping-away of divisions, that she advocates. It is not, of course, only women writers who can cross academic and disciplinary barriers; Lacan and Derrida can both find a place (if for 'literature' one reads 'psychoanalysis' and 'philosophy' respectively) under each of the four headings above, and under none of them. But where feminist writing has most spectacularly marked its distance (which is inevitably a political one) from the traditional academic institution is in its refusal of the consensually 'correct' neutral vantage-point for the reading of texts. This is not of course true only in France, as the work of a Kate Millett or an Elaine Showalter demonstrates; gender-neutrality has been shown to be as much of a chimera in reading a text as ideological or cultural neutrality. Where French feminism makes perhaps its most original contribution is in the distance it takes from the specifically French canon of avant-garde writers. This – not codified in one critical work as with F. R. Leavis's *The Great Tradition*, but the product of the hegemony of *Tel Quel* and Roland Barthes over French critical counter-orthodoxy – included such writers as the Marquis de Sade, Georges Bataille, Robbe-Grillet, the nine-teenth-century 'pre-surrealist' Lautréamont, and even such 'establishment' figures as Nietzsche and Baudelaire, seen as subverting the ortho-dox canon from within. A writer such as Benoîte Groult is no more in awe of such names than is Kate Millett of the supposedly liberating potential of many modern British and American writers. Groult's account of the Baudelairean attitude towards female sexuality bears some resemblance to American feminist denunciations of Henry Miller or D. H. Lawrence:

> the slit is the Devil: a hairy thing lying under a dress, a thing which lies open to filth and brings down the menstrual blood, the latter being the 'formless horror of violence'. . . . Desire is reduced to the taste for that which is dirty, degrading, and destructive, which is to say, for death.[15]

The context, however, is somewhat different. The connection between desire and death – a prominent theme in the work of Georges Bataille – is also important in the Lacanian schema, where its third term is language, so that Groult in this passage is actually turning a psycho-analytic discourse against itself, showing that the materiality of language so dear to it is not a safely containable theoretical concept, but can issue in destructive and ultimately fatal ways. Barthes and Sollers, at the time the effective King and Dauphin (or 'Clown Prince' . . .) of the 'new criticism', are fiercely criticised later in the article for the praise they lavished on what for Groult are works of 'the most banal sadism',[16] such as *Justine* or *Histoire d'O*. Her work – and the same can be said in different ways of such writers as Marguerite Duras or Annie Leclerc – thus takes as one of its main targets the male-dominated field of 'new' literary theory, a field informed and inhabited by many of the thinkers considered here.

The impact of feminist writing in France has thus not been confined to the values of 'objectivity' and 'neutrality' associated with the academic Right; the battle has been carried into the heart of the counter-orthodox camp, through a questioning of the whole concept of the ideological efficacy of texts. *Tel Quel's* politics of the signifier provided a sophisti-cated theoretical justification, claiming descent from the sacred duo of Marxism and Freudianism, for the radical liberating possibilities of the texts it exalted.

Benoîte Groult and others deflate this by the simple expedient of pointing out that it is only possible to read those texts unquestioningly in that way if you are male, which leads variously to the conclusion that theory (and *a fortiori* what became known as 'grand theory' or 'Theory', the ambitious kind of systematisation attempted among others by *Tel Quel*) is a phallocratic enterprise of totalisation, or that feminism needs urgently to elaborate theories in its turn. The armoury of concepts brought to bear on the texts Theory has chosen to promulgate is stopped in its tracks by the cry: 'We are here – what about *us?*' To the arrogance of much theoretical work, if not to its intricacy, feminist writers have provided the most devastating counterblast.

8　Language, Power, and Politics – the Work of Foucault and Deleuze

Virtually all the work dealt with up to now has been overtly political, in its context and its frame of reference. The next two chapters look at work of a somewhat different kind, whose relationship to the political struggles of post-1968 France is often implicit or ambiguous, so it will be helpful briefly to pause and draw together some of the main threads that have run through the work hitherto.

Most significant of these for what follows is the re-definition or re-evaluation of what constituted the 'political'. The joyful overleaping of old barriers in May, the Althusserian theorisation of the 'three instances' (economic, political, and ideological), the spiritual exhortations of a Garaudy, the ethically-based commitment of a Sartre, the manifold repercussions of the 'new' psychoanalysis and feminism for the politics of everyday and family life – all contributed to a movement which no political institution could afford to disregard or theory to ignore. What became almost literally unthinkable in the wake of this was the idea that there might be spheres of human conscious activity not necessarily dominated by the political. The life-style of the most disciplined Maoist cells (illustrated and parodied in Jean-Luc Godard's *La Chinoise* of 1967) was indeed so designed as to make such an eventuality impossible, through the literal lack of any time or place into which it might fit itself.

That the political was everything was a principle difficult to sustain for very long, as well as being a highly questionable development of the notion that everything was at least in part political. Language, as the last chapter showed, was a major focus of intellectual discussion here, if only because it was the medium in which that discussion took place. The view of language implicit in the traditional academic institution (an expression that in this context runs the gamut from a Sorbonne lecture to a Lagarde and Michard manual) had been that it was a transparent, value-free medium for the transmission of ideas and information. That it might necessarily involve and rework questions of sexuality, ideology, and the unconscious was a notion deeply disturbing in its implications. If language has thus emerged as one major thread, another – more destructive still of established institutions and practices – is that of *power*, and it is to the articulation of the two in the work of Michel Foucault that we shall first turn.

Much that is dealt with thereafter (in particular the work of Derrida) may seem to dispossess power and reinstate the unchallenged conceptual sway of language in a politically equivocal manner; but the implications of this work for the (political and pedagogical) institution will be shown to be as disturbing as those of Lacanian psychoanalysis or Foucaldian historiography for the institution(s) in and against which they were written. Once the repressed of a psyche, a society, or a discourse has been brought to light – on a couch, on a barricade, in a factory or a university, in a textual or a pedagogical practice – there can be no consistent turning-back from it.

Foucault's work can best be understood here as an extension of those limits, thus paralleling the 'spirit of May' and its aftermath. At a time, just after his death, when there is a large-scale assessment of his work as epistemologist and theoretician (a term that will need qualification), it is important to redress the balance by pointing out that his major impact on the French Left since 1968 came through the areas he examined, rather than the concepts he deployed to examine them. It is not, of course, possible entirely to disentangle the two, but with that important reservation it is still meaningful to say that Foucault's political significance lay in the attention he gave to areas often considered politically as well as socially marginal – madness, imprisonment, the medical clinic, the origins of our ideas of and on sexuality.

In this respect he can be seen as developing and extending the work of the *Annales* school of French history, which grew up around a review founded by Marc Bloch, Fernand Braudel, and Lucien Febvre in 1929. The trademarks of this school can be summarised as close attention to areas previously considered outside the scope – or beneath the dignity – of professional historians; a rejection of *l'histoire événementielle*, the presentation of history as a chronicle of events or 'watersheds'; and a concentration rather on the economic, social, and physical climate of a historical period – what Richard Cobb has summarised as 'medicine, disease, plague, weather, death, love, arson, and so on'.[1] In all these ways it bears much similarity to work in local, cultural, and oral history in Britain and the USA.

One striking difference, however, is in the degree of institutional prominence. Ever since the end of the Second World War, there has been a strong connection between *Annales* and the Sixth Section of the École Pratique des Hautes Études – a leading institution for social-science research, and (after Barthes's appointment there in 1962) renowned as a stronghold of structuralism. In 1974 the Sixth Section attained separate status as the École des Hautes Études en Sciences Sociales, whose President since 1977 has been François Furet, one of the leading *Annales* historians. Foucault himself was never a 'member' of the *Annales* school, nor of the staff of 'Hautes Études' (he went from the philosophy faculty at the University of Clermont-Ferrand to a chair at the Collège de France), but the conception of history in his work is very similar to theirs, and the political implications of this have been among his major contributions to left-wing intellectual life. The death of Pompidou – de Gaulle's 'dauphin' – and his replacement by Giscard led to widespread criticism and revaluation of the Resistance, the main founding myth of Gaullism, to which Foucault contributed with an interview on 'La mémoire populaire' ['Popular memory'] in a 1974 issue of *Cahiers du Cinéma*. Films such as *La Chagrin et la Pitié* [*The Sorrow and the Pity*] – a documentary montage directed by Marcel Ophuls – and Louis Malle's *Lacombe Lucien*, about a young peasant from the South-West who collaborates with the occupying Germans, were seen by Foucault as repossessing and rearticulating a particular 'memory' of the Occupation period that had been repressed so as to become almost literally unthinkable by the hegemony of Gaullism. Foucault saw 1968 as the moment after which popular struggle moved from the domain of 'folklore' to that of the 'possible'; but it was not only the larger public traumas suppressed by *l'histoire événementielle* that interested him. In 1973, he edited and presented the confessional statement of a young Norman peasant who had murdered his bullying mother, and his brother and sister, in the 1830s. *Moi, Pierre Rivière, ayant égorgé ma mère, ma soeur et mon frère* [*I, Pierre Rivière, having slit the throats of my mother, my sister, and my brother*] – the opening words of the confession – attracted widespread attention, and was filmed in 1975 by René Allio, using non-professional actors some of whom were actual descendants of the characters they played. Foucault's comment on this was: 'Because Allio chose to commemorate this act on virtually the same location and with almost the same characters as 150 years ago, the same peasants in the same place make the same gestures again.'[2] This rests on a ritualistic view of 'history as re-enactment' which cinematic theorists have strongly criticised for its 'confusion of human persons with political agents'.[3] That a more dialectical analysis of the production of historical discourse

would undoubtedly have been possible is at once true and beside the
point being made here, which is that Foucault was bringing into the
domain of history an area that – certainly before the *Annales* school –
would have been relegated to the *fait divers*, the journalistic realm of the
'human interest' story.

The creation of a place in the French cultural formation for voices and
histories that had up till then been marginalised or excluded had
important political implications (particularly in the 'post-post-Gaullist'
period of the early and mid-seventies); but these were less contemporary, though probably more far-reaching, than Foucault's intervention in the Bruay affair. This took the form of a debate (published in
Les Temps Modernes) with Maoist militants, and the divergences
between Foucault's political stance and that of self-styled 'Marxist–
Leninists' emerge strikingly. The Maoist justification for the setting-up
of 'people's courts' to try the Leroy case and others in parallel is that 'to
make the revolution, there has to be a revolutionary party, and for the
revolution to keep going there has to be a revolutionary state apparatus'[4]
– an argument of impeccable Leninist pedigree. Foucault's retort was
based on his work on institutions of containment, both medical and
juridical, which had led him to point to the continued existence of structures of repression as a major problem that even a revolutionary appropriation of state power would not necessarily solve. To quote Barry
Smart, in Foucault's work: 'the question of the institutional form of the
state has been de-centred in preference for an analysis of the particular
individualising techniques of power and cultural modes of objectifi-
cation to which human beings in modern societies have become
increasingly subject'.[5]

Thus it is that Foucault criticises the 'alternative courts' set up by the
Maoists for perpetuating divisions that are necessarily repressive. For
him 'the revolution' (it is unclear, in a very *soixante-huitard* way, exactly
what this would mean) 'can only take place via the radical elimination of
the judicial apparatus, and everything that might bring the penal
apparatus to mind, everything that could re-introduce its ideology and
allow that ideology to creep back surreptitiously into popular practices,
must be banished.'[6] He expresses particular unease about the way in
which the 'Lens Tribunal', through its very structure and disposition,
'reconstitutes a kind of division of labour' (here, between 'judges' and
'public')[7], thereby reinforcing the bourgeois fallacy that a court of
popular inquiry can somehow unearth 'objective truth' under the aegis
of left-wing intellectuals imported specifically for that purpose.

Twelve years later and more, this entire debate may appear politically irrelevant, even embarrassingly so. The weaknesses of the Maoists' position has already been commented upon, and Foucault's global condemnation of anything that even looked like a state apparatus is all too easily pilloried as utopian and anarchistic. But this is to disregard the very real impact of the debate at the time – the manner (however maladroit) in which it drew attention to the flagrant inequalities that pervaded the French judicial system, and to the manifest incapacity to discover the facts of the case that at least partially stemmed from that.

It is also to take Foucault's observations in too literally political a way – an easy thing to do, if only because he himself seems to be doing so in this interview. An extremely important context in which to read much of his work is the French intellectual and artistic tendency to take a sympathetic, and at least implicitly political, interest in the criminal: as existential outcast, rebel against society, and even moral philosopher. De Sade, Baudelaire, and the major philosophical influence on Foucault, Nietzsche, are key texts here. So too is the minor nineteenth-century poet Lacenaire, something of an epigone of the Marquis de Sade. Lacenaire, who lived by crime and was guillotined for murder, appears as a character (superbly played by Marcel Herrand) in Carné's *Les Enfants du Paradis*. More importantly for our purposes, he fascinated Dostoevsky, who is supposed to have based Raskolnikov in *Crime and Punishment* partially upon him; and Dostoevsky was more widely read in France in the 1930s and 1940s than anywhere else in Europe. Gide's conception of the *acte gratuit*, embodied in Lafcadio's 'motiveless' murder in *Les Caves du Vatican* [*The Vatican Cellars*], was of Dostoevskyan origin, and his work is a major reference-point too for Camus in *Le Mythe de Sisyphe* [*The Myth of Sisyphus*].

At an interesting tangent to this anarcho-existentialist view of the criminal-as-hero is the affair of the Papin sisters, which occurred in Le Mans in 1933. Two inseparable sisters who worked as maids for a bourgeois family set upon their mistress and her daughter one night, after a mild reproof for domestic negligence, tore out their eyes, battered them to death, and mutilated the bodies hideously. That such a case should inspire reflection and analysis is hardly surprising, but what is significant here is that its repercussions were both literary and theoretical. The playwright Jean Genet (himself a criminal, analysed by Sartre in *Saint Genet*) based *Les Bonnes* [*The Maids*], probably his best-known work, upon the case; and two of Lacan's first articles – published in 1933 in the surrealist magazine *Le Minotaure*, and reprinted with his thesis as *Premiers écrits sur la paranoia* [*Early writings on paranoia*] in 1975 – also dealt with it. It would be quite wrong to say that for either

Lacan or Genet the Papin sisters were 'heroic' in the same way as Genet himself was for Sartre or Raskolnikov for Gide, but it should be clear that their case fits into the same overall pattern of fascination. Foucault's interest in Pierre Rivière, and later in the contemporary criminal-turned-novelist Roger Knobelspiess, can likewise be understood in this context. If 'criminals' are simply men or women who happen to find themselves on the wrong side of a dividing-line imposed by society, and shifting from one social formation to the next, then the whole panoply of bourgeois justice, with its archaisms of dress and behaviour suggestive of timeless verities, is a grotesque misrepresentation, and the criminal, by resisting and opposing it, can be seen as a kind of political hero. The political conclusions Foucault draws here are less important than the reasons for which he draws them.

Much has been written about Foucault's relationship to Marxism, often by Marxists clearly anxious to claim him as one of theirs. His activity in prisoners'-rights groups, his candour about his homosexuality and rejection of the normative family structure, and the stress much of his work places on returning to the 'people' the voices and institutions supposedly stolen from them, all indicate an evident left-wing stance, but any attempt to present this as a Marxist one runs into Foucault's own denials and his rejection of the possibility of any comprehensive theory or science. In *L'Archéologie du savoir* [*The archeology of knowledge*], he contrasts his post-Nietzschean epistemology (described first as 'archeology', then as 'genealogy') with the totalising, and thus dominative, pretensions of Marxism, which is invested with 'the effects of a power which the West since medieval times has attributed to science and has reserved for those engaged in scientific discourse'.[6] For Foucault, it might be said, the theory of theories – how they appear, are enunciated, gain credibility, and then after a period of time disappear – is a possible object of study; but Theory itself is a chimera. Power, already mentioned as a key Foucaldian concept, is what is at stake here. Theory, whatever its claims to liberate, can only do so by imposing itself – through, that is to say, the exercise, or at least the threat, of coercion. The political implications of this are ambiguous, as can be seen from the different bodies of work that refer to Foucault: the warmed-over humanism and suspect spirituality of the 'new philosophers', but also Bourdieu's analysis of the educational process as rooted in 'symbolic violence', and the evolution of Poulantzas in his last work, *État, pouvoir, socialisme*, away from a structuralist perspective towards an emphasis on the pervasiveness of State power at all levels of society, in self-styled 'socialist' systems no less than in capitalist ones.

Power recurs as an important motif in Foucault's last work, *Histoire de la sexualité* [*History of sexuality*]. This was intended to consist of six volumes, the first of which appeared in 1976; that only three have been published (though a fourth is apparently being prepared for publication) is not solely the result of Foucault's death, for there was an eight-year gap between the first volume and the second and third which Foucault explains in his 'self-criticising' introduction to the second volume.

The greater prominence of intellectuals in France has meant that their revaluations or recantations of previously-stated positions have greater news-value than those of their British counterparts. Sartre, with his stress on authenticity and the writer's ethical obligation to make his/her positions publicly known, was a key figure here. The concept of self-criticism was also at the beginning of our period an important one for Marxist (especially Maoist) militants, for whom it was meant to show the constant renewal of correct political awareness; the work of Althusser, notably *Éléments d'autocritique* [*Elements of self-criticism*] and *Réponse à John Lewis*, can be seen as an amalgam of the two types of self-criticism, reflecting his dual role as Marxist and as intellectual figure.

Foucault's 'self-criticism' (though he does not call it that) comes closer to the Sartrean tradition of public questioning of one's own premises. The first volume, *La volonté de savoir* [*The will to knowledge*], had set out to overturn the idea that Western bourgeois society sought to disavow or repress the production of sexuality. On the contrary, for Foucault, it has been marked by the proliferation of discourses on sexuality (and we should remember that in his terms the *concept* of 'sexuality', as opposed to the activity of sex, can only be produced in discourse). 'Man, in the West, has become a confessional animal';[7] the link between sexuality, confession, and the third term of power, established by the Church and reworked in texts as varied as Rousseau's *Confessions* and *My Secret Life* by the Victorian writer 'Walter', is a central theme of Foucault's study.

La volonté de savoir was severely criticised on its publication, for the sweepingness of its conclusions and the sense that Foucault was manipulating the data to fit an interesting but perverse (and not praiseworthily so) initial hypothesis. In the Introduction to Volume II, *L'usage des plaisirs* [*The use of pleasure*], Foucault reiterates his statement in the earlier volume that sexuality is not an invariant human quality whose mutations can be accounted for simply by the different types of repression used at different times. The very constitution of sexuality, in other words, as well as its repression, partakes of the omnipresence of power. How his analysis in this and the third volume, *Le souci de soi*

[*Care and concern for oneself*], differs markedly from *La volonté de savoir*, is thus explained by Foucault:

> After the study of truth-games in relation to one another . . . and then of truth-games in their relation to power, another kind of work seemed to become necessary: to study truth-games in one's relationship to oneself and the constitution of that self as a subject, taking as sphere of reference and field of investigation what might be called 'the history of the man of desire'.[8]

It is, in other words, the manner in which the 'game'[9] of truth, language, and power goes to constitute the individual desiring subject that is Foucault's prime concern in these two volumes. Thus it was that the scope of his study broadened to encompass what he calls 'the slow formation, during the Classical period, of a hermeneutics of self'.[10] *L'usage des plaisirs* deals with this in ancient Greece, *La souci de soi* in Rome.

The two volumes were greeted with a critical reception as enthusiastic as their predecessor's had been hostile. This has a great deal to do with the exhaustiveness of Foucault's research and the blend of empathy and scholarship that (particularly since the rise to prominence of *Annales*) has been the touchstone for historians in France. Foucault delved deeply into philosophical, historical, ethical, and physiological works to support his contention that the classical period, far from being a riot of pagan hedonism, was actually marked by considerable rigour and reflection on the subject (in both senses) of sexuality. The titles of the two volumes suggest how for Foucault the exercise of sexuality fitted in Greece into a more general 'personal economy' involving all other aspects of an individual's life in society, and in Rome (where there was less public participation in civic affairs) into an 'intensification of the relationship with oneself'[11] that already called into question the barrier between public and private.

We have seen that one major area of left-wing intellectual activity in modern France has been the whole question of how individuals are constituted as 'subjects' in society. Althusserian Marxism, Lacanian psychoanalysis, and their conjunction in the textual politics of Barthes, Sollers, and *Cahiers du Cinéma* are the best-known bodies of work in this area. Foucault's development in the two later volumes of *Histoire de la sexualité* fits interestingly into this context, even though the names of Marx and Freud – never mind Althusser and Lacan – figure nowhere in the work. Where Foucault finds common ground with the work of

Theory in this area is in the importance attached to the relationship between sexuality, subjectivity, power, and language. Where he diverges, however – and this is more significant – is in his exclusive concentration on texts contemporary with the period he is discussing. In the late 1960s and early 1970s, this would doubtless have been criticised as empiricist; but the dwindling credibility of Theory has led to changes in the intellectual climate, hardly anywhere figured more prominently than in *L'usage des plaisirs* and *Le souci de soi*. Foucault's use of contemporary sources is of a piece with his insistence, from *Histoire de la folie* onwards, of the need to read each historical period in the light of its own discursive and epistemological principles – principles that only a reading of the period, through what is has excluded or marginalised as well as what it has found acceptable, can reveal. The major interest of these last works in this context lies in Foucault's reconstruction of the sexual subjectivity of bygone periods, and its political implications, without reference to a vocabulary that at one time might almost have seemed the only one possible.

A work often associated with Foucault, largely because of his enthusiastic endorsement of it, is *L'anti-Oedipe* [*The anti-Oedipus*], by Gilles Deleuze and Félix Guattari, both teachers at the University of Vincennes. The interest of *L'anti-Oedipe*, more strikingly than of any work considered hitherto, resides in its reception and impact as much as in the ideas it elaborates. Denis Kambouchner is harsh, but symptomatic, in describing it as the first example of 'a short-term philosophical production, where ideas perish like vegetables and go out of fashion faster than clothes'.[13]

Kambouchner undoubtedly had in mind the 'new philosophers', some of whom (notably Jambet and Lardreau, authors of *L'ange* [*The Angel*]), worked within an explicitly 'Deleuzian' perspective; but beyond this his observation relates back to the changes in the intellectual market already remarked upon. For readers coming from the British philosophical tradition, with its stress on solid 'factual' inquiry and the empiricist rooting-out of truffles of certainty, such changes, and the phenomena to which they give rise, will appear frivolous, exhibitionistic, and devoid of any claims to serious intellectual standing. (The savage criticisms levelled at Derrida by the Berkeley philosopher John Searle, an Oxford graduate, repose, in part implicitly, on this attitude.) For those from what was until recently the dominant literary tradition, with its 'Leavisite' horror alike of intellectual fashion and of philosophy, the culture-shock occasioned by a phenomenon such as *L'anti-Oedipe* will be still greater, though doubtless attenuated by the recent efforts of such writers as Stephen Heath or Terry Eagleton to bridge the epistemological Channel. What is important here is to see the 'nine-days'-wonders' characteristic of French intellectual life not as somehow embodying Gallic moral inferiority, but as likely (though perhaps not inevitable) concomitants of the much more central place ideas and intellectuals occupy in French society and culture. It may appear perverse to assert that it is because the French take their intellectuals much more seriously that those same intellectuals are able to don what for an Anglo–Saxon public is the garb of brazen frivolity, but such a paradox at least makes some attempt to take stock of the very real differences between French and Anglo–American culture, by enabling even meretricious intellectual artefacts to be treated as though they had some diagnostic value.

This is emphatically not to say that *L'anti-Oedipe* is meretricious, merely that there are other ways of dealing with the rapid obsolescence of much of it than ethical condemnation or embarrassed silence. There are similarities between some of the arguments developed by Deleuze and Guattari and those of the British exponents of anti-psychiatry such as R. D. Laing and David Cooper, most notably in the writers' championing of the schizophrenic as social subversive. But Laing and Cooper, working within an existentialist perspective, use very different terms from Deleuze and Guattari, whose vocabulary stems from a post-Nietzschean 'vitalist' tradition (it is noteworthy that Deleuze has written on both Nietzsche and Bergson). The unconscious, for them, is not a theatre in which the same dramas are constantly enacted, as it is for Freud and Lacan. Rather, it is an assembly of 'desiring machines', whose disparateness and irreducibility are passed over by psychoanalysis in favour of a normative retelling of the same (Oedipal) tale.

It is possible here to recognise elements of the Foucaldian refusal of Theory. Like Foucault too (at least in his earlier work), Deleuze and Guattari take a bold macro-historical view, detecting beneath superficial changes and similarities fundamental shifts that issue in different relations of the unconscious's 'fluxes of desire' to the objects around it. Pre-capitalist or peasant societies 'encoded' their production of desire on the land, which became something like a collective or communal fetish. The encoding of desire in the feudal system was on the person of the monarch, while capitalism's inherent potential for revolutionary change rests in its 'decoding' of the mechanisms of libidinal energy. These need no longer be fixated on an individual object, and might thus, in breaking free from the 'love-objects' such a society puts before them (of which money is the most important), institute a polymorphous 'new order' whose structuring principle would be its very disorder.

Psychoanalysis, alas, is the fly in the ointment:

> Abstract subjective Work, as represented in private property, has as its correlative abstract subjective Desire, represented in the 'privatised' family. Psychoanalysis takes care of this second term as political economy does of the first. Psychoanalysis is the applied technique whose axiomatic is political economy . . . . The ambiguity of psycho- analysis in its relation to myth or tragedy can be explained in this way: it undoes them as objective representations, and discovers in them the figures of a universal subjective libido; but then it rediscovers them, and puts them forward as subjective representations which raise their mythical and tragic contents to infinity.[14]

In other words, apart from its alleged normative insistence that the plethora of unconscious pulsations are really 'just the same old story', psychoanalysis is guilty of putting forward universalising representation that tie up psychic energies in a manner ultimately beneficial to the capitalist order. This does not mean, of course, that Deleuze and Guattari's work is not throughout influenced by it; their view of libidinal investment in 'part-objects' – mouths, anuses, breasts – has much in common with that of Melanie Klein, a psychoanalytic writer more widely available and appreciated in France than in Britain (Derrida is the husband of her French translator). And it is none the less valid for being perhaps facile to play the *tu quoque* card against them by pointing out that many of their criticisms of Lacan ('The three errors on desire are called lack, the Law, and the signifier. They are one and the same error, an idealism which forms a pious conception of the unconscious'.[15]) smack of the very theoretical intransigence with which they reproach him, and – more tellingly – of a fixation or 'encoding' on him of their desiring impulses as writers similar to that Lacan constantly sought to induce in those around him.

To the 'neuroticising' process of psychoanalysis, Deleuze and Guattari counterpose what they call 'schizo-analysis', whose task is 'to assemble the desiring machines that interact with each individual and group him together with others'.[16] The institutional focus for much work of this kind was the Clinique de la Borde, at Cour-Cheverny in the Parisian suburbs, with which Guattari is connected. This clinic (as Sherry Turkle mentions in *Psychoanalytic Politics*) seems to have promoted a somewhat romanticised view of the schizophrenic condition, whose privilege is seen by Deleuze and Guattari as 'political and epistemological rather than moral and aesthetic, as for Laing'.[17] It is this romantic quality that has most obviously dated in *L'anti-Oedipe*, whose glorification of the schizophrenic could well be subject to the same kind of criticism feminists have levelled at the Barthesian eulogy of de Sade and others.

This is not to deny the importance of Deleuze and Guattari's undermining of the old-school Marxist distinction between base and superstructure, in which they rejoin (ironically) the very tendencies against – though also out of – which they write. If 'desiring production is as much part of the base as social production'[18] – if indeed desiring production *is* a form of social production – much the same can be said of the materiality of language in an Althusserian or Lacanian schema. Precisely because it deploys many similar concepts, but in a self-consciously atomised rather than totalising fashion, *L'anti-Oedipe* now appears as an important intervention against the hegemony of Theory which by 1972 was well-established. With the undercutting of that hegemony, the text's force as counterweight ceased to be so significant, and, lacking in the conceptual force of a Foucault (who if he had written it would doubtless have attempted some explanation of what a 'desiring machine' actually is), *L'anti-Oedipe* may now appear as little more than a rhetorical excursus. It is, however, part of the premise on which *this* text is based that rhetorical excursuses, especially when their impact is so rapid and so considerable, are for that very reason well deserving of contextual study. *L'anti-Oedipe* remains an important part of the intellectual landscape of its time.

9 Language, Literature, Deconstruction and Politics

The writers discussed in this chapter, widely different though their work is, have one major feature in common – their central preoccupation with language. This is an important concern of all the thinkers mentioned in this study, but with each chapter thus far it has become more and more central. Debray, Sartre, the various Marxist philosophers all in different ways take 'society' (or aspects of it) as their area of exploration, and language for them is often, though not always, seen as the means to this end. (Sartre's renunciation of fiction in favour of more militant political involvement can be read as a deliberate 'acting-out' of this view.) For Lacan, the relationship between language and his object of study, the processes of the human psyche, is more complex, for one can quite literally not be said to exist without the other. The distinction between 'means' and 'area' of exploration comes to seem as untenable as that once staunchly upheld between 'form' and 'content' in literature. Irigaray, Foucault, Cixous, Deleuze all take as their object of study the relationships between power and language, so that in their work the political and the linguistic (not without friction or ambiguity) coalesce. *Tel Quel* articulated this coalescence in a prescriptive (sometimes autocratic) way; it is explored, as briefly mentioned in the last chapter, by one of their principal contributors, Julia Kristeva.

The very title of *Semiotike – recherches pour une sémanalyse* [*Semiotike – researches towards a semio-analysis*], especially on the cover and title-page where the word *'semiotike'* appears in the original Greek letters, figures one of Kristeva's main concerns, with non-contemporary and non-Western modes and systems of signification. This was certainly connected with her Sinophilia, as the texts she produced after visiting China (*Des Chinoises* [*About Chinese women*] and the *Tel Quel* article 'Les Chinoises "à contre-courant"' ['Chinese women "against the stream"'], both in 1974) clearly show; but it had also to do with a more general cultural and political interest in how ideas on language, politics, and subjectivity drawn from a rereading of Marx and Freud might be applicable outside the canon of modern Western texts. *Semiotike*'s sometimes bewildering bombardment of references – to medieval courtly texts and blazons, classical and neo-classical rhetoric, Greek philosophy, the use of gesture in Oriental signifying systems – is thus a quite deliberate textual strategy (though none the less bewildering for that).

It links in too with Kristeva's stress on language and textuality as *production*. The concept is here understood in a specifically Marxist sense:

> The great novelty of Marxist economy was, it has several times been emphasised, that it thought of the social as a specific *mode of production*. Work ceases to be a human *subjectivity* or *essence*. Marx replaces the concept of 'a supernatural creative power' (*Critique of the Gotha Programme*) with that of 'production', seen in a twofold light: the labour-process and the social relations of production, whose components belong to a combinatory scheme with a logic of its own. One could say that the variations of this scheme are the different types of semiotic *system*.[1]

Marxist literary theory tends, by analogy with the economic process, to see 'supernatural creative power' as a bourgeois disguise for the relations of production – textual, linguistic, and economic – on which any text is based (cf. Macherey's *Pour une théorie de la production littéraire*). The notion that vocabularies supposedly the province of other disciplines (such as economics) can – sometimes must – be used in the analysis of literary texts is thus basic to Marxist-influenced criticism, but Kristeva carries it a great deal further by incorporating into her discourse terms drawn from classical rhetoric, sign-language, and even (like Lacan in his later work) mathematics, of which she says:

> As the product of a logical, rationalistic abstraction, linguistics finds it difficult to be sensitive to the violence of language as movement across an area in which, in the pulsation of its rhythm, it sets up its significations. We really need a mathematical formalism to make 'monological' science more flexible and to lay bare the skeleton, the grapheme of the organisation in which the dialectic of language is realised: an infinity of uninterrupted ordered permutations.[2]

The stress on the Marxist view of language as system of production as well as of exchange, and that on the need to bring mathematics to bear on the flux and flow of language, both suggest the desire for a *science* of criticism (in the sense in which Marxism claims to be a science of society) which animated the work that went on around *Tel Quel* in the late 1960s and early 1970s. Schematically, it is possible to say that later work in this area – notably that of Lyotard, considered in Chapter 10 – concentrates on the *desire* for a science of criticism rather than on that science itself, seen as a chimera much as Theory is for Foucault. Kristeva's work thus functions as an important pre-text for much that came after, which is not to belittle it but rather to apply to Kristeva herself the concept for which her work is best known, that of *intertextuality*. This foregrounds the impossibility of considering a text (as formalist critics in particular are prone to do) as a self-contained whole, and the necessity always to read it in its relationship with other texts. Kristeva explains how this ties in with her stress on production:

> The text is thus a *productivity*, which means: (i) that its relationship to the language in which it is situated is redistributive (destructive–constructive), so that it can be approached through logical rather than purely linguistic categories; (ii) that it is a permutation of texts, an intertextuality: in the space of one text several utterances, taken from other texts, criss-cross and cancel one another out.[3]

This at once opens up the text to theory (which has as much right to inhabit it as any other discourse), and opens up theory (including Kristeva's own) as a text in its turn to be read in conjunction with other texts. The convolutions of this approach, in which text and intertext often seem no more truly separable than the two sides of a Möbius strip, are marginal to our purposes, but the political implications of inter-textuality (like those of its subsequent avatar, deconstruction) are important to an understanding of contemporary French intellectual life.

In the first place, and paradoxically in a text which if it now seems dated is so through the very insistence of its scientificity, Theory no longer appears impregnable on its throne. The 'sacred texts' are brought constantly into contact with other texts, from other cultures or disciplines, and such intertextual encounters as it were inevitably change both partners. Secondly, the text-as-monolith (the view implicit in bourgeois critical orthodoxy) is fissured, if not shattered, by the omnipresence of intertextuality. The pedagogical implications of this are certainly far-reaching, for the text is no longer a shrine at which to worship, or (the corollary approach) a finite file of data which the sufficiently painstaking or gifted scholar can one day hope to 'unpack'.

The Siamese twins of information and wonderment can no longer dominate the universe of criticism.

None of this is to deny, however, that the sophistication of this work textually was simply not matched by sufficient *political* sophistication. To assert that the political was everywhere, even to try to 'put politics in command' (Mao *dixit*) in one's own theoretical practice, was not an adequate base from which to grasp contemporary political reality. This is not to reiterate the inane cliché that 'intellectuals', by definition, can never have an adequate grasp of the 'real world'. Rather, it is to point out that if the economic, the ideological, and the political are indeed three spheres each endowed with its own 'relative autonomy', then a command of only one of them is hardly sufficient to produce knowledge of the social formation. The tendency of 'textual socialism' to delude itself that it was, was perhaps as fundamental an error as that which, for Althusser, the Hegelian Marxists made in asserting that Marx took the idealist dialectic and turned it upside-down. An engagement with the specificity of the different levels, in both cases, is what is missing.

This is figured in Kristeva's 1978 article in *Tel Quel*, 'La littérature dissidente comme réfutation du discours de gauche' ['Dissident literature as a refutation of left-wing discourse']. The impact of Solzhenitsyn upon the French intellectual Left has already been mentioned, and was certainly instrumental in leading both Kristeva and Sollers away from Marxism. For the moment, it is enough to note the exclusively linguistic – one might even say aesthetic – frame of reference Kristeva adopts. The polyphony of proper names in *The Gulag Archipelago*, comparisons with Diderot and Céline, references to the Menippean satire and the Bakhtinian 'carnival' – the analysis is a rich and stimulating one, but its political legitimacy, bearing in mind that it forms part of an effective public recantation by a former Maoist, is surely dubious. 'Coming from the future, the dissidents point to the worm in the fruit, and deprive the West of its bright new tomorrow'[4]; the implications of this discourse point towards a reactionary pessimism no more anchored in the French social formation of its time than was the text-based Marxism from which it sprang.

It may seem surprising that Roland Barthes is even included in a survey of the French intellectual Left since 1968. The socio-critical thrust of his earlier work is plain to see, though certainly not such as to earn him the label (*pace* John Ardagh) of 'Marxist'.[5] But during our period he moved away from the explicit social concerns of *Mythologies* and *Le degré zéro de l'écriture* [*Writing degree zero*], to produce work which many would not see as 'political' at all. This, however, is to disregard the major post-1968 shift in the idea of what constituted the 'political'. In that light, Barthes's 1970s' texts appear as remarkable 'signs of the times', so that while it would be a misrepresentation to describe him as expressly committed to the transformation of French society, it would be no less of one to pass over his work here. Barthes's difficulty in engaging with politics was, as he states in the 'autobiographical' text *Roland Barthes par Roland Barthes*, primarily of a linguistic order:

The discourse of politics is not the only one that repeats itself, spreads itself, becomes tired: as soon as a change takes place in discourse anywhere, there follows a vulgate and its exhausting procession of motionless phrases. If this common phenomenon strikes him [Roland Barthes] as especially intolerable in the case of political discourse, it is because there repetition takes on the appearance of a *climax*. Politics claims to be the fundamental science of reality, and we in our imagination endow it with an ultimate power, that of taming language, boiling all chitchat down to its residue of reality. How can we then accept uncomplainingly that politics too should sink back into the ranks of language, and turn into Babel?[6]

It is for Barthes the *doxa*, the ossification of sense(s) into common sense or of critical ideas into orthodoxy, that is the enemy to be fought, and this makes it possible to read his distaste for the 'vulgate' of political sloganising as more than the genteel outcry of an affronted sensibility. His major works of criticism frequently refuted the academic and pedagogical *doxa* of their time; thus, for instance, *S/Z* overthrew the accepted notion that the 'correct' way to read Balzac was as the apotheosis of large-scale literary realism, and many of the critical essays and *Le degré zéro* placed *Bouvard et Pécuchet* at the centre of the Flaubertian oeuvre and the beginning of 'modern' writing. The stultifying effects of a politics trapped in *doxa* had been plain to see in the PCF of the 1950s and 1960s, and Barthes's rejection of the 'exhausting procession of motionless phrases' appears more politically pertinent if read in this context.

Annette Lavers has pointed out that another major Barthesian work, *La plaisir du texte* [*The pleasure of the text*], belongs identifiably to the period of *L'anti-Oedipe*, 'with its scepticism about the development of history, its sexual language, its questioning of all norms'.[7] It would be possible to go further and see in Barthes's championing of Gide an important key to his sexual politics. Just as for Gide (homo)sexuality was released from the exigencies of reproduction into the liberating pastures of 'availability' (*disponibilité*), so for Barthes writing was to be set free – utopianly so – from the tyrannical demands of (a single) sense into the unbounded world of an infinite interweaving of senses. This is doubtless why Barthes was able to respond with a suspicious degree of aesthetic satisfaction to the political volte-face (or 'oscillations') of Philippe Sollers, in *Sollers écrivain* [*Sollers the writer*]: but, perhaps more importantly, it also figures (and is figured in) his distinction between 'encratic' discourses (those that are situated within power) and 'acratic' discourses, situated outside it.[8] The apparent frivolity and hedonism of his later texts – often seen as betokening a 'swing to the Right' – is best understood in this light. The study of the major redoubts of institutional power became tedious for Barthes through the monolithic sameness he attributed to it. It is '*le* politique', the political area in its widest sense, including notably the politics of the body and those of everyday life, that retains Barthes's interest in the later texts. '*La* politique', politics in the narrower, more 'specific' sense, through its inexorable encratic quality, had come to seem a sphere in which there was nothing new for him to say.

The political implications of the work of Jacques Derrida are currently the focus of much debate. His deconstructive readings of texts both philosophical (Husserl, J. L. Austin), and literary (Edmond Jabès, Philippe Sollers) – sometimes, as with Hegel and Genet in *Glas*, literally both at once – have had great, and continuing, impact, in the USA perhaps even more than in France; but their 'frame of reference' may seem to be resolutely apolitical, more so than for any of the other texts we have considered. Why, then, should this body of work attract ideologically and politically charged attention?

One reason is that Derrida has never made any secret of his own political sympathies. At the inaugural meeting of the Groupe de Recherche sur l'Enseignement Philosophie (GREPH), in 1976, he declared himself to be a Communist; he has actively worked for dissident philosophers in Czechoslovakia; his support for the French Socialist government has been unwavering; and it was that same government that made available the funds for a long-cherished project of his, the Collège International de Philosophie. This holds regular lectures and seminars to which philosophers from all over Europe are invited to contribute; its distinguishing mark is that admission is free and unrestricted – a truly 'Open University' of philosophy, with all the pedagogical and political implications that entails.

Derrida, then, is more overtly associated with the current French Left than almost any other leading philosopher; yet this is not accompanied by any *overt* political discourse in most of his work. The problems this poses are one obvious reason for the discussion it has aroused; another is that Derrida's intellectual constituency has tended, in France at any rate, to be on the Left. His work, in its constant and far-reaching interrogation of the bounds and possibilities of language, has affinities with that of the thinkers dealt with in this and the previous chapter, whom we have seen are generally on the Left in one way or another. The presumption, then, would probably be that Derrida was likewise, but this is less apparent from a reading of his work. Michael Ryan both identifies a major reason for this and suggests a way through it in saying that Derrida's analysis is 'confined to concepts and to language rather than to social institutions'.[7] This is certainly true if by 'social institutions' we understand, for instance, the form of the State, or the structure of the family; but what if the ultimate 'social institutions' without which no discussion or even articulation of these would be possible were, precisely, concepts and language? Such a presupposition both underlies and springs from an attempt to read Derrida's work politically.

There are two important texts in which Derrida addresses himself to explicitly political questions. One is a searching series of interviews published in 1972 under the title *Positions*, which like almost any Derridean title is a play on words. The 'position' of the subject in language, or of the reader in the text, was a key concept in French critical theory at this time, but the title also suggests that Derrida is to be asked to define and defend positions of a more explicitly political order. This is what happens when Jean-Louis Houdebine presses him on the possible relationship between his decentring of Western metaphysics and the Marxist concept of dialectical contradiction. Derrida's response is elusive, allusive, illuminating:

I do not believe that there is a 'fact' that enables us to say: in *the* Marxist text, *the* contradiction, *the* dialectic escape, *the* dominance of metaphysics. On the other hand, you say, following Lenin, that [matter has] the 'unique property' of 'being an objective reality, of existing outside our consciousness'. Each element of this proposition poses, let us admit, serious problems. We have to question all the residue handed down from the history of metaphysics . . . Wherever and in so far as the motif of contradiction is effectively operative, in textual work, outside a speculative dialectic, and taking into account a new problematic of meaning . . . I subscribe to it. You see, to repeat myself, I do not believe that one can speak, even from a Marxist point of view, of a homogeneous Marxist text that would immediately free the concept of contradiction from its speculative, teleological or eschatological horizon.[8]

Derrida is here saying that the Marxist concept of contradiction is a valid one only in so far as its validity is not accepted as transcendental proof of itself. To elevate any concept (be it 'contradiction', 'uniqueness', or even 'reality') to the status of unquestioned epistemological or political touchstone is to fall back into the trap of Western metaphysics since Plato and thereby to undercut the materialist basis of Marxist philosophy at the very moment one might appear to be asserting it.

This in turn leads to the hypothesis (confirmed by Derrida in these interviews and elsewhere) that, if he has remained perhaps puzzingly silent on Marx, this is because he has not (yet?) produced the kind of rigorous reading required to show how Marxist texts are no more exempt than others from the constant process of slippage and self-contradiction that for Derrida characterises all language. Christopher Norris puts it thus:

> That consciousness can be present to itself in the light of pure reason, delivered from the snares of opaque textuality, is a recurrent dream of Western thought. It is deeply embedded in the Marxist theory of text, ideology and representation, even where that theory is meticulously purged of crude deterministic thinking.[9]

Deeply embedded, to be sure, but, for Derrida, not nearly so deeply as in the obscurantist metaphysics of bourgeois philosophical and political rhetoric. The siren-song of deconstruction – at least in its depoliticised American versions – can lure the unwary reader onto the rocks of textual and ideological nihilism, but a careful scrutiny of Derrida should be enough to obviate that risk. The philosophical heritage he takes as his prime object of criticism is the heritage in which the self-legitimating claims of authority (that of a General de Gaulle apostrophising the French nation no less than of a Plato yearning for his ideal) throughout Western history have been grounded. Derrida's insistence that such transparent self-evidence can be shown to be destructive of itself thus has profound political implications, in a twofold sense. They are far-reaching, but/because they lie very deep.

Derrida addresses himself to the political constraints on the French educational system in *Où commence et comment finit un corps enseignant* [*Where a teaching body begins and how it ends*], published in the collection of essays *Politiques de la philosophie* [*The politics of philosophy*]. The GREPH and its parallel organisation, the Comité de recherche sur l'enseignement philosophique (Committee for research into philosophical teaching), were set up largely to counter the pressures for a downgrading of the importance of philosophy-teaching in France exerted by the Giscard regime. Derrida here describes his work as 'the (affirmative) deconstruction of phallogocentrism as philosophy'[10] – the dispossession, that is to say, of the 'Father' as fount of all knowledge through a close attention to the inconsistencies any articulation of this position must imply.

Power is not, for Derrida as for Foucault, simply a force brought to bear on the educational system from without, for the teaching body has a power of its own: 'that which it exercises in the very place from which it denounces power'.[11] This illustrates well how a deconstructionist approach, highlighting the internal contradictions of a discursive position, can thereby have direct political relevance. Derrida is both posing the question that has haunted politics since its inception – how can one do away with power other than by the exercise of it? – and evoking the way in which any educational system rests on what Bourdieu calls 'symbolic violence'. It is to the politics of power endemic in the education system that Derrida here draws attention. It is noteworthy too that he singles out, as the group most likely and best placed to criticise the institution of the university, the *maîtres-assistants* and *agrégés-répétiteurs* (the middle or 'career' lecturer grades). This gives rise to some characteristic punning observations on the importance of repetition as mainstay of pedagogical and linguistic systems, but to see only this would be once again to underestimate the subtle relevance of Derrida's political thrust. Until 1984 (when he was appointed to a professional post at 'Hautes Études'), he was himself a *maître-assistant* at the rue d'Ulm, so he writes here from within the very *garde* he singles out – as doubtless its most celebrated and influential member within the sphere of philosophy, but as a member of it none the less. Thus it is that his observations on the *maîtres-assistants* – neither so subordinate that they cannot afford to antagonise those in power, nor so well-placed within the system that they have everything to lose from changes in it – can be read as a justification of his own critical stance, and (in the hostile context of Giscardian France) as a call to others similarly placed to share it. *Où commence et comment finit un corps enseignant* is the text that most clearly illustrates the political implications of Derrida's work and the places where it was carried out.

These places are at once textual and pedagogical, which makes it possible to understand how Derrida's juxtaposing of German high thinking (Hegel) and French low living (Genet) in the parallel columns of *Glas*, or his inscription of a British linguistic philosopher (J. L. Austin) into 'Continental' discourse (*Signature/Événement/Contexte* [*Signature/Event/Context*], in *Marges de le philosophie* [*Margins of philosophy*]), have a particular political value in the France of today. The philosophical orthodoxy of the 1950s and 1960s, grounded in phenomenology and an idealist version of the dialectic, is the tradition in which Derrida was educated and against which he writes. The stress on heterogeneity and the play of difference in his own writing can be seen as an attempt to prevent it from solidifying into a similar 'tradition' of its own, though a moment's deconstructionist reflection will point to the trap lying in wait here: what is the place of authority from which a text can decree its own author's death-as-Father . . .?

For Michael Ryan, in *Marxism and Deconstruction*, the implications of deconstructive criticism debouch onto a non-hierarchical, non-Leninist style of 'new Left' politics, of a kind whose impact in post-1968 France is plain. The rejection of the necessary submission to the Father (at the root of Derrida's critiques of Lacan); the ruthless paring-away of the metaphysical, that repressed that returns so consistently across the history of 'materialist' philosophy; the refusal of a reductionist reading of any text (including that of History); the undermining of the claims to legitimacy made by contemporary Western institutions; the insistence on plurality and heterogeneity – these certainly offer striking parallels with the grounds on which the various 'new lefts' parted company with the 'old Bolshevism'. It would be possible, and not (only) perverse, to go one stage further and point to the similarities between Derridean views of textual inexhaustibility and the major tendency in recent political economy. If any reading of a text is necessarily blind to certain major aspects of it (an idea developed by 'post-Derridean' writers in the USA, notably Barbara Johnson and Paul de Man), then any indication of such 'blind spots' will itself be blind to aspects of the text upon which *it* is commenting – and so *ad infinitum*. . . . This is to suggest not merely that texts are inexhaustible, but that they breed in captivity at an expanding rate. The more written, the more remains to write. The textual 'multiplier' thus put into effect suggests that the political economy of deconstruction is Keynesian in its operation. That Derrida's own work has political implications of a more specifically left-wing kind emerges more clearly when it is considered in the context of the France of its time.

In the first interview ('Implications') published in *Positions*, Derrida says of *difference/differance* (the 'differing' of one phoneme or word from another assimilated to the 'deferring' of meaning across textual space) that it is 'the most general structure of economy, provided that what one understands by that is something other than the classical economy of metaphysics or the classic metaphysics of the economy'.[12] To read this as a metaphor would be misleading, for it would imply that the 'economy' in its financial sense was logically prior to the textual economy of production and distribution, rather than being one particular instance of it. This may seem to undercut the traditional Marxist stress on the primacy of the economic, but for much contemporary French thought that primacy has been, paradoxically, marginal; the 'determination by the economic in the last instance' has often been little more than an incantatory prelude after which the economic has been banished to the wings, while the political and the ideological in all their contradictory glory have occupied the centre of the stage.

The work of Derrida, and perhaps even more that of Jean-François Lyotard, can thus be seen as a re-instatement of the economic, in its omnipresence as much as in its specificity. For Lyotard, any discourse is the focus of (a number of) desire(s) – of a libidinal economy, according to the title of one of his best-known works – whose affects as they meet and collide carry the text simultaneously towards and away from the stasis of 'meaning'. Where his most striking political contribution lies is in the importance he attaches to the plurality of discourses, which may appear a classic liberal–democratic attitude but becomes something quite different in Lyotard's work.

The title of *Dérive à partir de Marx et Freud* [*A drift away from Marx and Freud*], a collection of texts previously published between 1968 and 1971, is revelatory. Lyotard is concerned, not with the synthesis of the two discourses which Theory attempted, but with the ways in which both drift from a unity of meaning towards a plurality of which he says: 'The plural, the collection of singularities, this is precisely what power, kapital [*sic*], the law of value, personal identity, identity-cards, the University, responsibility, the family, and the hospital curb and repress.'[13] The litany of repressive institutions is reminiscent of the kind of discourse that was widespread in May 1968, but Lyotard had been working along these lines for many years. During the 1950s and early 1960s, he had been an active member of the group Socialisme ou Barbarie [Socialism or Barbarism], led by Cornelius Castoriadis and Claude Lefort – a coalition of former Trotskyists and Communist dissidents strongly hostile to the international Communist movement from what after 1968 would have been called a *gauchiste* perspective. The group's critiques of state bureaucracy (which included Leninist party organisation), its espousal of workers' control, its philosophical rejection of Marxist claims to meta-theoretical supremacy: all are themes that either came to the fore during the 'events' or were developed as a result of them. The group came to an end in 1965, when the journal from which it took its name made its last appearance, but it has attracted a good deal of posthumous attention thanks to the May events and their aftermath.

Lyotard's long essay on Marx in *Dérive à partir de Marx et Freud*, 'La place de l'aliénation dans le retournement marxiste' ['The place of alienation in the Marxist inversion'] reinstates, against Althusser, alienation as a valid Marxist concept, for reasons not dissimilar to Lefebvre's, notably that it is 'the expression of a theoretical need if not an element in a theory'.[14] Lyotard's emphasis throughout these essays – whether he is analysing the manner in which teachers and academics are exploited in bourgeois society or critically assessing psychological and psychoanalytical modes of artistic and literary criticism – is on what cheats, thwarts, blocks, or undercuts totalising attempts at unification, from Left or Right. The text can desire and attain a non-contradictory unity of meaning only as the human psyche can desire and attain death; it is the point of irrevocable stasis and repose. It is thus the contradictory play of desire, even with such canonical bodies of work as Marx or Freud, that is figured in the title and foregrounded by the text of *Économie libidinale* [*Libidinal economy*].

The opening chapter, 'La grande pellicule éphémère' ['The great ephemeral film/tissue'], seeks to overthrow any idea of textual – *a fortiori* theoretical – fetishism, in favour of a generalised polymorphousness reminiscent of that proposed by Deleuze and Guattari in *L'anti-Oedipe*. Lyotard's work, however, differs sharply from theirs in the incisiveness and imagination with which it analyses major texts, above all Freud and Marx. The 'libidinal economy' of these texts is to be found in their fascination (unavowed, but available to analysis, just as is the unconscious) with those very areas and objects that they seek to denounce, abolish, or bring under control. Thus, for Freud, the death-drive – that which lies *Beyond the pleasure principle* – can never be fully recuperated into the systemic economy of psychonanalysis, and this is the source of the seductive power it exercises. Lyotard's approach to psychoanalysis is one of the few seriously to take into account the economic circuits it activates, which he describes thus:

The first, when the patient pays to reactivate his *jouissance*, and thus to metamorphose it into money; the second, when he speaks or tries to speak desire, and thus commutes it into concepts; the third, when the work of authoritative fixation upon sex is supposed to bring about the institution of a normal body, where libido will be sexual and sex genital, synonymous with the promise of reproduction.[15]

For *jouissance*, money; for desire, concepts (or even Theory); for polymorphousness and individuality, genital heterosexuality and the reproduction of the family – psychoanalysis as a system of exchange (and given the price of a session in Lacanian Paris it is hard not to think of it as that) is shown to have much in common with the other modes of exchange bourgeois society uses to regulate itself and its members. It is worth stressing that Lyotard's texts are deeply impregnated with Freudian concepts ('libidinal economy' itself is one) and that it would be a travesty to read his work on psychoanalysis as entirely negative. It derives its force here from the context of a time at which the widespread infatuation with Lacan's work in particular often went to obscure its normalising, not to say coercive, aspects.

In the chapter, 'Le désire nommé Marx' ['Desire called Marx'] Lyotard likewise brings to light the unacknowledged aspects of Marx's attitude towards capitalist exploitation – the 'libidinal geography of the [Marxist] continent', as he puts it.[16] Marx is seen as, on the one hand, wildly jealous of the capitalist-as-procurer, as systemic integrator, and, on the other, a small girl ('la petite Marx'), scandalised and horrified by relationships of exploitation and yearning for a golden age of socio-economic virginity when they will never have been. Thus:

> He [Marx] has to carry out the task of procurer which is assigned by his desire to integrate goods, services, and human beings into one body, his desire for genital harmony.[17]

But:

> The young 'she-Marx' says: I am in love with love, all this industrial and industrious shit must come to an end, that is my anguish, I want a return to the (in)organic body; and she is relieved by the great scholar with his beard, who lays it down that *it cannot fail to come to an end,* and, as the spokesman of the wretched (who include the little 'she-Marx'), puts forward his revolutionary conclusions.[18]

This obviously relates to Marx-as-text, not to the Karl Marx who was born in 1818 and died in 1883; but its relevance goes beyond, to the scandalised prurience and voyeuristic envy which Lyotard detects beneath the ethical earnestness and craving for theoretical integration prevalent among intellectuals on the Left. Beneath the 'scientific', one might say, the 'utopian' (as with 'the little "she-Marx's"' dream of undoing history), is still at work, and with it a concealed envy of the capitalism at once analysed and execrated. Is the integration of social and libidinal economy promised by Theory, after all, not a mere epigone of that triumphantly accomplished by the maraudingly normalising armies of capitalism on the march?

For Lyotard, then, while the founding claims of Marx and Freud are indispensable, Theory's claims to unification and homogenisation smack of the very system against which it purports to be working. The political implications of this become clearer in *La Condition post-moderne* [*The post-modern condition*], a report commissioned by the Universities Council of the Government of Quebec. The central issue it tackles is one that has underlain much of the work we have looked at here, from Althusser's distinction between science and ideology through to Foucault's epistemological investigations: the question of how know-ledge is legitimised. Lyotard's distinctive contribution is that he recognises the need for even the most rigorous scientific epistemology to provide some legitimising narrative of its claims. He refers to the 'incommensurability between popular narrative pragmatism, which provides immediate legitimation, and the language game known to the West as the question of legitimacy – or rather, legitimacy as a referent in the game of inquiry'.[19] In other words, the claims to truth made by 'popular narrative' – a fairy-tale, a folk-remedy, but also a daily newspaper or a detective novel – are implicitly self-validating in a way not available to would-be scientific discourses. Such discourses have tended to ground their claims in one of two 'master narratives': that of *totalisation* or that of legitimation. The first tells its hearers that the goal of scientific inquiry is the amassing of the totality of knowledge, the second that 'the truth shall set you free', that knowledge is the necessary precondition for liberation.

For Lyotard, neither of these claims is self-evidently true, for 'the . . . discourse that inaugurates science is not scientific, precisely to the extent that it attempts to legitimate science'.[20] This view, which derives from 'game-theories' of language such as those of Wittgenstein, also has much in common with Bertrand Russell's paradox about whether a set (of concepts, discourses, or whatever) can or cannot be a member of itself. A legitimising discourse or narrative is subject to the same kind of scrutiny as any other, and Lyotard's stress on the polyvalence of discourses means that his scrutiny of the two master narratives is destructive of their claims in the post-modern era. We have already seen that his work shows a profound mistrust of totalisation, and his deconstructive analysis of the Marxist intellectual in *Économie libidinale* points to a similar mistrust of the liberating narrative. It is difficult to think of a French philosopher since Sartre who, while remaining firmly of the Left, has been so acutely aware of the 'bad faith' that is a necessary component of the progressive intellectual's position.

What lies beyond the two narratives is, not a meta-meta-narrative that can outstrip and recuperate them in its turn, but a plurality of discourses, of ways of producing proof and of being right, figured at every level of post-modern society. This has clear affinities with the redefinition of the political that has constituted one of the 'master narratives' of this study; the multiplicity of discourses on the French Left since 1968, many of which have little in common in any way save that they claim to be 'socialist' and hence to speak some part of the 'truth' about (French) society, is the best possible illustration of Lyotard's thesis.

To the multiplication of language-games and 'micro-narratives' there corresponds the spread of the new technologies – home computers, data banks, and the other paraphernalia that, as in Thatcher's Britain, have tended to be the province of the political Right. There are clear ideological reasons for this, grounded in the stress on the *private* (the family unit, the 'freedom of the airwaves', the fetichisation of property) characteristic of the contemporary Right. But Lyotard puts his own notion into practice by finding a different kind of proof, a new way of being right. For him, the spread of technologies can also mean the spread of alternative language-games, and thus of an infinity of 'micro-politics' mounting a plurality of challenges to the centralising, normalising propensities of late capitalism:

> The line to follow for computerisation ... is, in principle, quite simple: give the public free access to the memory and data banks. Language games would then be games of perfect information at any moment. But they would also be non-zero-sum games, and by virtue of that fact discussion would never risk fixating in a position of minimax equilibrium because it had exhausted its stakes. For the stakes would be knowledge (or information, if you will), and the reserve of knowledge – language's reserve of possible utterances – is inexhaustible. This sketches the outline of a politics that would respect both the desire for justice and the desire for the unknown.[21]

It is possible, in the light of doubts about the confidentiality of databanks or the political implications of cable television, to find Lyotard's conclusion a trifle sanguine; but *La condition postmoderne's* articulation of the omnipresence of language-games with the spread of the new technologies makes it one of the most important texts of its time. It comes as no suprise to discover that Lyotard's contribution to the debate about the 'silence of the left-wing intellectuals' bears the title *Tombeau de l'intellectuel* [*Grave of the intellectual*], nor that in spite of that it is far from being a pessimistic or defeatist text. Lyotard maintains that the 'intellectual' as traditionally understood is an anachronism, who can be apostrophised in discourse but has no real social existence. The plurality of functions in post-modern society has replaced the unitary (one might almost speak of 'organic') intellectual by a series of executives, creators, decision-makers, citizens, and so forth – functions that can co-exist in the same individual at the same time, but without ever coalescing into the all-embracing figure of whose line Sartre was the last. It is the necessary incommensurability of post-modern linguistic regimes, which means that social conflicts are frequently 'settled' 'in the idiom of one [party], while the wrong done to the other is not even signified in that idiom',[21] that has driven the totalising project of the old-style intelligentsia into a marginality that is not even utopian, but simply nostalgic. *Languages*, rather than language, are for Lyotard the major ideological arena of post-modern society.

10 The 'New Philosophers'

The phenomenon known as the 'new philosophy' has attracted attention in Britain and America principally as the most extreme recent example of supposed Gallic modishness and perfidy. The term was coined in June 1976, when *Les Nouvelles Littéraires* published a dossier entitled *Les nouveaux philosophes* [*The new philosophers*], edited by the writer who was to become the most prominent of their number, Bernard-Henri Lévy. 1976 and 1977 saw a profusion of books, articles, public lectures, seminars, and radio and television appearances by such figures as Christian Jambet, Guy Lardreau, Philippe Némo, Jean-Marie Benoist, Jean-Paul Dollé, and André Glucksmann: all more or less associated with the 'new philosophy', despite Glucksmann's rejection of the label. The speed with which so may previously unknown writers became – at least briefly – celebrities was unprecedented, and widely criticised for being more akin to the marketing of film-stars or pop-singers than to the diffusion of serious ideas. Even François Aubral and Xavier Delcourt's trenchant critique of the movement, *Contre la nouvelle philosophie* [*Against the new philosophy*], itself widely diffused amid much publicity, was not immune to such criticism.

By the final years of the seventies, the phenomenon was markedly on the decline. Of the writers mentioned above, only Lévy and Glucksmann continue to attract attention; the others are famous only for having been famous, as though in proof of Andy Warhol's assertion that a time would come when everybody in the world would be a celebrity for five minutes. That the whole phenomenon was largely a media *coup*, engineered from the publishing-house Grasset for which Lévy works as a series director, and facilitated by the institutional channels Debray describes in *Le pouvoir intellectuel en France*, is not open to doubt; but simply to dismiss it as that is to ignore or underestimate those factors in the political and intellectual climate of the middle and late 1970s that made it possible for the 'new philosophers' to gain credence so rapidly.

There was a strong sense of *déjà vu* about those ideas, if not the manner in which they were diffused. The hostility to Marxism, as inescapably a philosophy, and a practice, of domination; the stress on the individual as repository of authentic values; the hankering after an often ill-defined spirituality: these all had much in common with the anti-Communist tendencies among the Parisian intelligentsia in the late 1940s. Raymond Aron's resignation from the editorial board of *Les Temps Modernes* and subsequent championing of the capitalist powers in his editorials for *Le Figaro*, and the vehement anti-Communism that as much as any sense of ethnic loyalty prevented Camus from condemning the French during the Algerian War, were the historical precedents that the new philosophers (the quotation-marks, for reasons of space, will henceforth be dispensed with) more or less consciously followed in what was in many ways a very similar period. To the discrediting of the USSR by the 1949 revelations about the death-camps corresponded the belated realisation of what the Cultural Revolution had really meant, and the PCF's loss of credibility in the early 1950s was matched by that of the late 1970s. In a more narrowly intellectual sense, the work of many of the thinkers we have discussed, with its stress on the connection between language and the mechanisms of power, had prepared the ground in which the ideas of the new philosophers could take root. Serge Quadruppani accounts for their rapid flourishing thus: 'As well as the Gulag effect and the Maoist legend, the new philosophy grounded its arguments in a conception of eternal power, fashioned from the writings of the two great master-thinkers of the French university, Lacan and Foucault.'[1]

Foucault's enthusiastic review of Glucksmann's *Les Maîtres Penseurs* [*The Master Thinkers*] in 1977 would seem to bear out this judgement, but as Aubral and Delcourt point out much of the new philosophy rested upon a highly partial and selective reading of the founding texts. From Lacan, it derived the notion of the omnipresent Master, who holds the keys of language and desire (a little like Lacan himself), a view particularly marked in Jambet and Lardreau's *L'Ange*. From the Maoist version of Marxism previously espoused by many of the new philosophers (including Lévy), the idea of oppression, in a heavily metaphysicalised version, is retained, and that of exploitation – its economic counterpart – elided or ignored. Similarly, Maurice Clavel, a predecessor and then a fellow-traveller of the group, is criticised by Aubral and Delcourt for misrepresenting Foucault in his *Ce que je crois* [*What I believe*]:

From Foucault's book *Les mots et les choses*, what has Clavel retained? A tawdry argument along the lines: 'no more man' for Foucault, 'so no more me, no more I to exist as still the same!' . . . 'How was it that I had to wait for Foucault to understand that I existed only through God, that the "I" is an article of faith, that nothing, neither the world nor my consciousness, guarantees its existence for me, that to speak of oneself there is only Faith, in which God causes me to be, and Revelation, in which God has told me that I am?'[2]

Foucault himself certainly never wrote anything to suggest that that was what he understood. Much of the hostility to the new philosophy on the Left sprang not only from the political coat-turning of many of its adherents, or their manifest media opportunism, but from a long French tradition (dating back at least to Descartes) of robust hostility to any suspicion of the metaphysical. This was undoubtedly strengthened by the dominance of a radical anti-clericalism in the educational world. The resulting attitude, whose tendency was often to impoverish thinking on the French Left, was, we have seen, implicitly rejected by much of what went on in 1968 and its aftermath, and that rejection unsurprisingly often took an excessive form in its turn. This comes through in such outpourings as Clavel's, and even more so perhaps in the following explanation by Jambet and Lardreau of their extravagant earlier embracing of the Mao Zedong cult: 'One normally comes into politics out of conviction, and as we all know that takes time. Whereas we plunged into the "Lin-Piao madness" at one fell swoop and, as Claude Mauriac said the other day, out of a taste for the absolute'.[3]

Beneath the veneer of revolutionary politics, then, what this particular band of lapsed Maoists discovered was a hunger for spiritual certainty little different from that to which Camus had given expression in his philosophical works. This was true even of Philippe Sollers, who while not a 'new philosopher' was closely associated with the group; his enthusiasm for the horizons of individual freedom he discovered on a visit to the USA went hand-in-hand with a recantation of his previous theoretical positions, fuelled by his encounter with *The Gulag Archipelago* and spelt out in a 1978 article in *Tel Quel*, 'Le marxisme sodomisé par la psychanalyse, elle-même violée par on ne sait pas quoi' ['Marxism sodomised by psychoanalysis, itself raped by . . . something or other']. The emphasis here is on the uncontainability and irreducibility of literature and art – now both seen as spheres about which neither Marxism nor psychoanalysis can have anything worthwhile to say. Marxism, for Sollers, is motivated by a 'rage to enslave that which lives and speaks',[4] of which Stalin's cultural policies and reflections on language were but the logical culmination. As for Freud, he 'merely ratifies in his own way a belief in the omnipotence of science in relation to art'; and all the para-scientific claims so confidently made by

the Sollers of ten years before now appear as having 'as their most fundamental, absolute, and secret desire the model of the Catholic Church'.[5]
The affinities between the Vatican and the Kremlin were not exactly
new matter for comment, though they had been given a fresh twist by the
tendency in 1960s France for the offspring of rich Catholic families to
turn towards China rather than the USSR for their socialist model.
Sollers's fundamentalist faith in Art as the Ultimate Mystery evokes the
vaporous elucubrations of a Bernard Levin rather than the mature credo
of a politically sophisticated writer and thinker, largely because that is
what he had never been. The Gulag revelations, like those about the
Cultural Revolution, obviously precipitated much rethinking on the
Left, but Sollers's reaction was so extreme as thereby to betray its own
facileness, and inevitably to discredit the *political* seriousness of his
textual practice.

The new philosophers, at least, had not made such vociferous public
claims to theoretical comprehensiveness (most of them had been too
busy in *khâgne* or preparing for the *agrégation* in 1968), and the attacks
on them, by Deleuze among others, had as much to do with their deriva-
tiveness and reliance on mass-marketing as with their political volte-
face. Lévy declared his support for Mitterrand in 1981, while at the same
time insisting on the need for the Left to break away from its commitment to 'socialism'. In the work that made his name, *La barbarie à visage
humain* [*Barbarism with a human face*], he goes so far as to write an
imaginary dictionary entry for the year 2000:

> Socialism: masculine noun, a cultural genre, born in Paris in 1848,
> died in Paris in 1968.[6]

The 'socialism' whose epitaph Lévy is pre-emptively writing is clearly of
a centralising, and thus in his terms totalitarian, sort. So narrow a view
did indeed 'die' in Paris in 1968, simply because it was never possible to
see it thereafter as the only possible pattern for the transformation of
society; but the alacrity with which Lévy sweeps away all other varieties
of 'socialism' along with it suggests at best a simplistic vision, at worst
calculating bad faith.

If Lévy's definition of 'socialism' as born and dying in Paris seems to
show at once a concentration upon French society and history and a
mistrust of it, the reasons underlying this become clear in *L'idéologie
française* [*The French ideology*] of 1981 – a text worthy of consideration
because it has made more impact than any other produced by a new
philosopher in the decade. What Lévy does here is to take ideas first put

into currency by the 'post-post-Gaullist' debate on 'popular memory' and the Resistance, and write them into a much wider context to suggest that the true 'French ideology' is one tainted by fascism. This was an understandable attitude in the France of 1980 – the year in which, as Lévy points out, a synagogue in the Rue Copernic in Paris was bombed the week before Jean Elleinstein began his collaboration on *Le Figaro-Magazine*. The electoral successes of Le Pen's Front National in 1984 provide disquieting proof that fascist tendencies are gaining in support. But Lévy's main concern is not the modern political implications of fascism; his self-appointed task is to bring deeper realities to light, notably that the influence of the fascist tradition in France has rarely been more pervasively exerted than in and through the PCF.

That Party's discourse and activity, as in its recent campaigns against the use of illegal drugs or the concentration of immigrants in working-class suburbs and shanty-towns, has often been characterised by a populism that feeds off many of the same anxieties as fascism. Lévy's juxtaposition of Thorez's 1940 article from exile with elements of Pétainist vocabulary, in an attempt to prove that the two are at bottom the same,[7] is, however, a fanciful 'scissor-and-paste' endeavour, and his pell-mell association of names and figures is rooted in a rhetoric as sweeping as that he condemns. What is important here is less Lévy's undoubted methodological weaknesses as what they tell us about the intellectual and political context in which he was writing – one in which the crisis of the Left, electorally and ideologically, had led to an intense self-examination which, particularly when it took the form of erudite self-recrimination, could be highly marketable. Lévy's denunciation of his compatriots and Sollers's tearing-up of his Maoist credentials both reflect an awareness of this, if often of little else. Lévy's assertion that the 'French ideology' has been largely impervious to foreign, especially German, influences is in contradiction with the thesis put forward by André Glucksmann in *Les Maîtres Penseurs*. The 'master thinkers' whose baleful influence is there denounced are the great Teutonic systematisers: Fichte, Nietzsche (seen as totalisor rather than deconstructor), and above all Hegel. To blame Hegel for the totalising propensities of Marxist philosophy, and hence at one or more removes for the totalitarian propensities of Marxist practice, was hardly novel; Camus had trodden that path a quarter of a century before in *L'Homme révolté* [*The Rebel*]. Glucksmann is more far-reaching still, seeing in the 'text' of German philosophy the seeds of all totalitarian evil, whether of 'left' or 'right':

The 'Germany' in which fascism was born is not a territory or a population, but a text and a textual relationship, instituted long before Hitler and diffused well beyond the frontiers of the Holy Roman Empire. That Germany is still with us; it is to be found in the modern brains of this modern planet, in the Pentagon in Washington as much as in some God-forsaken concentration-camp in the Cambodian countryside.[8]

The stress on the importance of textuality fits clearly into the intellectual setting of the time; Régis Debray, three years later, was to give a considerably more subtle development of the idea that 'a government is sustained, not only by the gun, but by the effects of texts upon others'.[9] For Glucksmann, the most pernicious of these effects is the creation of a group – which he calls 'the plebs' – that exists simply in order to be tamed and marshalled by the elite of 'master thinkers'. German philosophy, grounded in the elitism of the intelligentsia, provides it in its turn with a theoretical corroboration that tends towards the totalitarian:

Masters hand on power only to other masters. Not through ill-will or self-interest, but because power – of 'capitalism' or 'socialism' – remains the power to abstract, and because to abstract and to conceptualise is to dominate (Hegel). The master thinkers have never given us anything but delicate, subtle, and interminable observations from the point of view of the dominator; in their eyes, the dominated, trapped in their particularity, have no point of view.[10]

The possibility of non-elitist or non-hierarchical forms of socialism is one that Glucksmann does not seriously entertain, despite that fact that there was no shortage of available discourses for condemning totalitarian communism in socialist – even Marxist – terms. His privileged moments are those of disorder and unpredictability, which he finds even at the heart of so irredeemably ideological an event as the French Revolution:

The events of 89 in France, other, more scattered revolts down the centuries, from the first riots in Florence through to the 'dubious struggle' of workers before the New Deal, or the struggles of American blacks and students during the Vietnam War – all these disorders are more decisive than the musical chairs of governments or the determinants of the economic market.[11]

The assimilation of the French Revolution to May 1968, through the term 'the events of 89'; the smattering of New Left rhetoric ('the struggles of blacks and students'); the cavalier dismissal of electoral politics and the importance of the economic: these all go to suggest a self-indulgent political aesthetic, whose glorification of the marginal and the spontaneous is a superficial parody of the Foucaldian or deconstructionist rewritings of the political. In the year immediately preceding one of the most important general elections in France's history, its tenor could only give comfort to a Right which probably felt at the time that defeat was staring it in the face. Glucksmann's more recent diatribes against nuclear disarmament draw upon other (at least until recently) fashionable discourses – psychoanalysis, paradox and aporia, 'Gulagese' – to back up their governing notion of *dissuasion*, 'deterrence' in French but endowed at the same time with overtones of coherent rationality similar to those of 'dissuasion' in English.[12] 'Glucksmann's own position is wildly ideological, even by its own criteria'[13]; the wildness and the ideology are both present as far back as *Les Maîtres Penseurs,* and it is merely their rightward slant that has become more apparent.

11 The Place of Sociology

One theme that has run through this study has been the undermining of traditional disciplinary barriers by structuralist and post-structuralist modes of thought. We have seen how philosophy, literary criticism, linguistics, history, and psychoanalysis mingle in the key texts of the period, to produce what Richard Rorty has described as the 'new genre' of theory.[1] Almost entirely absent hitherto, however, has been the field of sociology – a surprising omission considering that in Britain (at least until theory made its major impact on literary and media studies, in the mid-1970s) it was propably the most important area of left-wing intellectual activity. Why has its influence in France, until recently at any rate, been so much less?

One reason is the dominance of the *concours* system (*agrégation* and *CAPES*) within French universities. The subjects that figure in the *agrégation* tend to be those taught in secondary schools – literature (classical and modern), foreign languages, philosophy – since the rationale of the competitive system is after all to fill vacancies as they arise. Possession of the *CAPES* or *agrégation* is the best guarantee of material security for a French academic, which means that to pursue a career in a non-*concours* area involves either considerable financial risk or an often complex process of self-recycling. Thus, many lecturers in non-*concours* areas such as psychology or sociology began their career by taking the philosophy *agrégation*, and only then moved into another discipline.

This in turn has tended to mean that the restructuring of French academic life since 1968 has taken the form of a redistribution between and within already existing subject-areas, rather than of the multiplication of new ones. Pierre Bourdieu in *Homo Academicus* illustrates the wider political implications of this through the 'demotion' of philology after 1968 and the corresponding 'promotion' of linguistics.[2] The already-mentioned attempt under Giscard to reduce the amount of philosophy taught in schools likewise shows how academic subject-areas could become the focus of political conflict. Such a climate was obviously not favourable to the promotion of sociology or psychoanalysis. There is a further reason for the comparative eclipse of sociology in the first part of our period, which has to do with the totalising claims made by (or on behalf of) Theory. Their thrust was inevitably antiempirical, for the construction of conceptual models (and, later, their deconstruction) was of prime importance. Obviously such models had referents out in the 'real world' of human social, economic, and psychic life, but the stress on the non-transparency of language, and the necessarily contradictory and opaque relationship between signifier and signified, or one signifier and another, tended to marginalise the importance of such referents. This is what lies at the root of, for example, E. P. Thompson's savage criticism of Althusser, grounded as it is in an intellectual tradition for which pragmatic inquiry is of the essence. When Theory, in the work of Derrida and others, began to turn back upon itself, one at first sight unexpected consequence was the re-emergence and re-instatement of pragmatism. This is because deconstruction, to quote Jonathan Culler, 'offers a similar critique of the philosophical tradition and emphasises the institutional and conventional constraints on discursive inquiry'[3]; it is thus no longer possible to speak of the Theoretical text as the key to scientific knowledge, for such a text can only exist in (a number of different) context(s), and cannot by hypostatised as the bearer of truth.

Between the deconstructive work of Derrida and the exhaustive empirical inquiries mounted by Bourdieu, there seems at first to be very little in common; but both currents in different ways arose out of the disillusionment with Theory already discussed, and both in different ways re-inscribe pragmatism into their practice. The two other important sociologists we shall look at here, Alain Touraine and Jean Baudrillard, appear to have very little in common either with Bourdieu or with each other, and one may begin to wonder what the disciplinary coherence of French sociology is, if indeed it exists. One answer to this is simply that such a coherence is nowadays as illusory as that of philosophy, literary criticism, or any of the other old disciplinary bottles into which the new, post-1968 wine was poured. Another is that Touraine's preoccupation with the 'new social movements' (like that of André Gorz, who provides a valuable point of comparison), Bourdieu's stress on the primacy of the body and the need for empirical inquiry into cultural practices, and Baudrillard's post-Nietzschean, post-Deleuzian nihilism are all part of the general disillusionment with Theory. It is not difficult to see how the claims made on behalf of Theory, as what Lyotard would call the ultimate legitimising narrative, necessarily tended to reinforce an attitude of aristocratic condescension towards more pragmatic domains of inquiry, especially when these occupied a subaltern place in the academic hierarchy. The work now discussed represents different aspects of sociology's revenge on Theory.

The more or less simultaneous appearance, in the spring of 1980, of Alain Touraine's *L'après-socialisme* [*After socialism*] and André Gorz's *Adieux au prolétariat* [*Farewell to the proletariat*] was a major event in French intellectual life. *Les Nouvelles Littéraires* described it as follows:

> Without ostentation or spectacle, the French intellectual Left is living through a real cultural revolution. Twelve years after 68, André Gorz and Alain Touraine, who for the past twenty years have incarnated the French idea of progress, bury without fuss the doctrine of socialism, and put it away on the shelf of outdated ideological accessories. Each writer, in his way . . . proclaims the extinction of a dominant ideology, in an attempt to replace it by a political thought better adapted to today's social changes.[4]

This account is clearly over-schematic, as an analysis of the two works' often very different approaches will show; but it does indicate how, in the year before the Socialists gained political control, a revision of what had hitherto been thought of as 'socialist' ideology was taking place not dissimilar to the 'Eurocommunist' revaluation within the communist movement. Like that tendency, the ideas of Touraine and Gorz both represent a movement away from the monolithic conceptions of the political party and the state apparatus, towards a re-insertion into the political vocabulary of the 'established' Left of many key ideas of May – on the importance of decentralisation, the death of what Touraine calls 'the Great Party', and the need for a new kind of approach to questions of production and consumption. Thus, Touraine points out that in what he calls 'post-industrial society', characterised by a move away from an industrial towards a technologically-planned economy, so fundamental a question as what productivity actually is needs to be re-posed:

> When we consume education or medical care, are we not also producing or reproducing our own productive capacity? The time is past when one could separate productive from non-productive activities, as if factories were productive whereas schools, hospitals, and administrative organisations were not.[5]

This has much in common with the defetichisation of manual labour favoured by the Eurocommunists and others, and figures in the

Socialist's successful subsequent attempt to win votes from the white-collar and middle-class electorates. Touraine's opening statement that 'socialist ideology no longer mobilises people'[6] is thus true only if socialism is understood in a narrow, and increasingly anachronistic, sense – in which case it comes to resemble a self-fulfilling prophecy. The Socialists' current political fortunes certainly show that it is much harder for them to consolidate support among the white-collar electorate; their haemorrhage of popularity, and Mitterrand's jettisoning of one socialist idea or scheme after another, like so many hundredweight of ballast, graphically illustrates this. But it is difficult at this stage to say how far this is a general proof of Touraine's assertion, and how far the product of more specific 'local' circumstances, such as the exaggerated hopes placed in the new government at a time of world recession and the internal friction, and eventual break, with the PCF.

The 'socialism' whose grave Touraine sets himself the task of digging is characterised in the first place by its State-centredness and lofty superiority to trade-union militancy. This latter has traditionally been far less important in French than in British politics, for reasons connected with the long-standing *étatisme* of French society:

Its [the State's] strength and arrogance, the splendour of its military – especially Napoleonic – traditions, the influence of the Catholic Church, likewise more ready to fight for convictions than for reforms, the superiority of the *grandes écoles* at the service of the State over the universities, closer to the bourgeoisie – everything has made of France ... a country where questions of history and the State appear more serious and exalted than the problems of the bourgeoisie and its enemies. So France has tended to be a country of State servants and petty-bourgeois, rather than of entrepreneurs and trade-unionists.[7]

This, for Touraine, means that the Left in France has tended to be pre-occupied with the capture of State power through its political parties, rather than with mass organisations such as trade unions. It is not difficult to see the importance attached to Theory as in some sort homo-logous with that attached to the State; both are centralising instances of social struggle. Touraine quite correctly points out that, in the aftermath of 1968 and the 'new social movements', such conceptions of political and ideological struggle are far too narrow. In this, many on the revolutionary Left would be at one with him, but Touraine sees them as bearers of the 'letter' of May against its 'spirit', in their sectarianism. It is interesting that two key episodes in the decline of the far Left singled out by

Touraine are the Bruay affair and the failure of the 1976 student strike. This, for him, provided the final refutation of the *gauchiste* notion that 'the problems of the university merely reflect those of the economic system'.[8] Again, as with his criticism of the outmodedness of State socialism, it is the movement's stress on centralism and integration that is Touraine's main target. Workers, students, and opponents of capitalism can no longer be expected to come together in a united opposition to the policies of a right-wing government – a point of view that might seem as destructive of the PCF's projected 'anti-monopolist alliance' as of the grandiose amalgamating sweep of *gauchisme*.

What is it, then, that Touraine advocates in place of these supposedly discredited models? His positive recommendations are coloured by the work's total failure (remarked upon by Max Gallo[8]) to take any account at all of the international dimension. Considering that two of the most important factors in French domestic politics since the election of the Socialist government have been the impact of the links between the PCF and the USSR on the one hand, and the world recession on the other, such an omission could well be felt to disqualify Touraine's work from serious consideration. His eulogy of the 'new social movements' (feminists, ecologists, anti-nuclear campaigners) gives very little idea of how they might relate to the larger power-struggles that he may deplore, but cannot unilaterally abolish. Such movements, for Touraine, clearly have history – even History – on their side, since the most important task now is 'to invent a *post-socialist* [my italics] and anti-*étatiste* Left';[9] yet the invocation of History to give a political position the performative force of inevitability is a favourite stratagem of that same 'traditional' Left Touraine is taking to task. What his discourse constantly hints at, without ever overtly embracing it, is the kind of eclecticism to be found on the left wing of the American Democratic Party or of the British SDP – a rhetoric of dynamic pluralism whose practical implementation would be likely to leave untouched the relations of production that dominate Western societies. Régis Debray, in a debate with Touraine in *Le Matin*, says that for Touraine 'social space has neither depth nor breadth, neither past nor enemies'[10] – a particularly telling criticism to make of a sociologist! – and goes on to draw a helpful distinction between the diagnostic and the prognostic aspects of the book: 'I believe that the Left needs lawyers more than prophets. The whole notarial aspect of your ideas pleases me, but their prophetic aspect I find frightening.'[11]

The title of *Adieux au prolétariat* suggests a tone no less prophetic than Touraine's, but there are significant differences between the two analyses. Gorz, like Touraine, is aware of the limitations of *étatiste* socialism, under which 'the taking of State power by the working class becomes in fact the takeover of the working class by the power of the State'.[12] And he shares the recognition that the traditional view of the industrial working class as the motor of social change is now outdated. But he is far less concerned than Touraine with scoring points off the political parties of the Left, and far more aware of the importance of relations of production and of the continuing need for the State to play an important role in many areas. His assertion that 'Keynes is dead', and that the alternative henceforth is between 'two ways of managing the abolition of work – one leading to a society of unemployment, the other to a society of free time',[13] may seem to contradict that, and to gesture wildly in the direction of Utopia; but it is precisely the delimited role of the State that points the way out of the apparent contradiction. For Gorz, modern society's 'pincer movement' of automation and unemployment tends to mean that the worlds of work and leisure become increasingly separate, and that individuals identify themselves less and less with and through the former. He sees this, not as an undesirable alienation to be overcome, but as a distinction endemic in modern social and techno-logical development, which nees to be fully recognised and pushed to its limits through the 'organisation of a discontinuous social space, made up of two distinct spheres and a life punctuated by the passage from one to the other'.[14] How can this punctuation and alternation be ensured? Clearly not by the 'society of unemployment', grounded in free-market economics, which is one of the alternatives Gorz postulates. The only forms of social organisation that for him are capable of doing without State regulation of what Marx called 'civil society' are those with a religious or quasi-religious focus, such as monasteries, kibbutzim, or communes (it is tempting to add revolutionary parties to the list). This is what lies behind Gorz's assertion – superficially similar to Lévy's, but quite other in its implications for political practice – that 'the themes of Fascist ideology are constantly present, in a diffuse form, in every layer and class of these [industrialised] societies, especially in the working classes (and, in France, in the discourse of the Communist leaders)'.[15] Such 'themes' include, for Gorz, the replacement of

> a system of functional domination by the permanent promotion of the most able, the power of a single class monopolising key positions by the personal power of the Führer, the State and its bureaucracy by mass organisations driven by a single thought and a single will.[16]

It may be objected that such a seeming equation of 'Communism' and 'Fascism' resembles the discourse often adopted by right-wing parties anxious to maintain and occupy the 'middle ground'; but the contextual thrust of Gorz's attack is, not just against the offensive and opportunistic populism of the PCF's tactics at the time, but against all those movements, of Right or Left, that might seek to replace State intervention by hypostatised charisma – of a General de Gaulle, a Mao Zedong, 'the masses', or whatever. The dominant necessity he perceives is for the State to ensure plurality in civil society by exercising its authority to plan and delimit.

Gorz's division between the 'sphere of necessity' and the 'sphere of autonomy',[17] idealistic as it may appear, is only so if taken as an essentialist statement. As a heuristic indication that there may be an alternative to the dead hand of *étatisme*, or the deceptive appeal of charismatic spontaneism, it distils well those aspects of the May movements that are still relevant to French political life in the 1980s. The criticism levelled at Touraine by Pierre Mauroy, in *Le Matin*, by its very inapplicability to the work of Gorz, serves to show the distance between the two: 'We can even see [in Touraine's work] the underlying idea that a bourgeois republic at least leaves the Left, kept at arm's length by the State, the freedom to imagine, or even to conquer, a few spaces of liberty. Whereas a "Socialist state" . . .'[18]

To open a copy of Pierre Bourdieu's *La Distinction* is to get an immediate impression of the difference between his work and that of other major French figures. *La Distinction* is copiously documented with statistics and analytical tables, and – even more unexpectedly for a 'theoretical' work – illustrated with a wide variety of photographs. The pragmatic connotations of the social analysis, like the frivolity at which the photographs of a working-class kitchen or a bean-eating contest hint, are likely to prove disconcerting. Is this social theory, or high-class journalism?

A Bourdelian reply to this might be to deny the separateness of the two, or at least to see the distinction as a re-enactment of the division between mental and manual labour which intellectuals of the Left frequently claim to deplore. The revenge of sociology upon Theory earlier referred to is perhaps Bourdieu's most important political contribution; Richard Nice distils it well:

The inclination to valorise the clinical, 'pure' activity of 'theoretical labour' and to denigrate the subaltern task of constructing and organising mere facts ultimately refers back to the division of mental and manual labour. It is no accident, Bourdieu argues, that the materialism which points too directly to historical and even biological determinations, short-circuiting the problematics of ideology and consciousness, is designated as 'vulgar'. This is the ironic resurgence of an aristocratic ideology of 'distinction', testifying both to the autonomy and to the dependence of the intellectual field on the field of class relations.[19]

Bourdieu's position thus has affinities both with Derrida when he speaks of the power the teaching body exercises 'in the very place from which it denounces power',[20] and with Debray's telling comments in *Le Scribe* on intellectuals' occupational blindness to the consequences of their privileged position for the very social groups for whom they profess concern.[21] He develops it, however, in a very different manner, neither playing with the aporia as Derrida does nor foregrounding a political ethics of authenticity like Debray. What he is above all concerned to do is to re-inscribe practical considerations – of biology, sociology, illustration, empirical inquiry – into a theoretical discourse that, in the wake of Lévi-Strauss and Althusser particularly, has loftily relegated them to an infrastructure to whose supposed dominance it pays at best lip-service.

We have already seen how the connotative resonances of the word '*corps*' have been much developed and exploited in contemporary French thought. For Bourdieu, these begin where they also end: within the individual body, which literally *in-corporates* the characteristics – of attitude, dress, comportment – of its owner's social position, so that social agents 'come to form *one body* with their social position'.[22] Gramsci's idea of hegemony stresses the ways in which the ruling class maintains its superiority through the acquiescence and consent of the dominated as well as through their repression. Developments of this on the European Left in recent years have tended to privilege the importance of culture and the superstructure, giving rise to what Nice in another context calls 'an intellectualism congenial to intellectuals'.[23] For Bourdieu, such hegemony would go beyond the cultural or even the conscious, to the most elementary and seemingly inevitable interiorisation of class position in the body and the physical environment it produces.

Nor is the economic neglected in his work as it is in so much left-wing thinking. Bourdieu sees the educational system, and indeed the whole superstructure of a society, as the place where economic capital is exchanged for what he calls 'symbolic' or 'cultural' capital, which can in turn be reconverted into economic capital in a multiplicity of ways which his work sets out to document and analyse. Here his analysis has much in common with Thorstein Veblen's theory of 'conspicuous consumption', whereby the manner in which individuals consume their wealth has to do with their desire to assert their social position (the coffee-table book, or the middle-class child's ballet lessons, are good examples of this). But it needs to be stressed again that right from his early anthropological work, Bourdieu is concerned with movement from the particular to the general – or in Marxist terms from the infrastructure to the superstructure. His theoretical positions derive from a constant empirical scrutiny into which they are fed back and to which they are constantly subjected. Alain Accardo gives a helpful summary of the major differences between Bourdieu's work and the previously dominant tendencies in Leftist critiques of 'ideology':

There is a tendency to ignore, or forget, that ideology is not reducible to ideas 'in one's head', but that it consists at least as much, if not more, of visceral feelings, implicit certainties, existential beliefs that are seldom if ever verbalised, a lasting style of being, feeling, perceiving, in short that it becomes flesh, blood, and body, and that in the form of incorporated dispositions and internal structures of subjectivity – in short, in the form of a *habitus* – it is capable of surviving for a long time the disappearance of those external structures of which it is the 'reflection', but the transposed, relatively autonomous reflection, living a life of its own and unendingly saying 'I . . . I . . .'[24]

The habitus is originally a medical term, denoting the general physiological 'shape' of an individual; it is significant that it should be from one of the biological sciences that Bourdieu borrowed his key concept. His most important work for us in the period under discussion (apart from *La Distinction*, which deserves extended discussion in its own right) is concerned with the structure and functioning of the French educational system, an area he first began to explore with Jean-Claude Passeron in *Les Héritiers* [*The Inheritors*] of 1964. It is in this short book that Bourdieu and Passeron first develop the implications of the aristocratic 'ideology of distinction' implicitly shared by students from the culturally and financially better-off sections of society, and much of what they say about the implicit contradiction between this and the secure professional future expected by the students foreshadows the events of 1968, certainly as they affected those students dismissed by the PCF as '*fils de papa*'.

Le Reproduction [*Reproduction*] (English translation *Reproduction in education, society, and culture*) provides an extended development of the ideas broached in *Les Héritiers,* and in so doing considerably sharpens their political focus. The earlier work argues for 'a genuinely rational pedagogy . . . founded on a sociology of cultural inequalities'[25]; *Le Reproduction* inserts its consideration of the educational system into a much wider view of 'pedagogic action', which is 'objectively, symbolic violence in so far as it is the imposition of a cultural arbitrary by an arbitrary power'.[26] This is not true solely of the 'old-school', mandarin style of education; even the most libertarian and participatory pedagogy cannot but rely upon symbolic violence for its maintenance, as Bourdieu and Passeron make clear:

> The term 'symbolic violence', which explicitly states the break made with all spontaneous representations and spontaneist conceptions of pedagogic action, recommended itself to us as a means of indicating the theoretical unity of all actions characterised by the twofold arbitrariness of symbolic imposition; it also signifies the fact that this general theory of actions of symbolic violence (whether exerted by the healer, the sorcerer, the priest, the prophet, the propagandist, the teacher, the psychiatrist or the psychoanalyst) belongs to a general theory of violence and legitimate violence, as is directly attested by the interchangeability of the different forms of social violence and indirectly by the homology between the school system's monopoly of legitimate symbolic violence and the State's monopoly of the legitimate use of physical violence.[27]

The affinities of this with the Althusserian 'ideological state apparatus', or Foucault's view that violence and exclusion are the basic preconditions of any discourse or epistemology, are more superficially apparent, but less fundamentally important, than the differences. What neither of these takes sufficiently into account is the complexity of the mechanisms by which the dominated interiorise consent to their domination, which for Bourdieu and Passeron is the major political role of the educational system in contemporary Western society. 'PAs [pedagogical actions] always tend to reproduce the structure or the distribution of cultural capital . . . thereby contributing to the reproduction of the social structure'.[28] This may appear nihilistic in its implications – for instance, that alternative or oppositional methods of schooling are at best drops in the ocean, at worst particularly nefarious forms of mystification. It does, however, have the advantage of attempting to account theoretically for the undisputed predominance of children from better-off and middle-class or upper-class families in higher education. For all the merits of

Althusser's essay, it provides no real developments of this; Althusser contents himself with such statements as that 'somewhere around the age of sixteen, a huge mass of children are ejected "into production"',[29] without exploring their implications. This is obviously in part because he was producing a concise essay in political philosophy, and not (like Bourdieu and Passeron) a full-length sociological treatise; but this in turn dispensed Althusser, as it dispensed so many other proponents of Theory, from the need to descend from the realm of the superstructural into the tiresome empirical determinants of the infrastructure. Bourdieu's importance in French intellectual life lies precisely in his insistence on the need to do this.

Homo Academicus, Bourdieu's survey of the French univerisity world, is a good example of this. Here he develops his notion that teachers and intellectuals are the dominated fraction of the dominant class (which gives concrete sociological form to their 'relative autonomy'), but is careful not to go on from that to hypostatise the whole profession as a single socio-economic force. It is not merely the position on the academic ladder that determines likely political affiliation, but also the individual lecturer's class origins and educational background, as well as the subject-area in which s/he works. Thus:

> What may appear as a kind of collective, organised defence of the professorial body is nothing more than the combined result of thousands of independent, yet orchestrated, strategies of reproduction, thousands of actions which contribute to the conservation of the body because they are the product of that social instinct of conservation that is a dominant habitus.[30]

Who or what orchestrates the various 'strategies of reproduction'? The answer is to be found in the underlying logic of the educational *field* - a term used, by analogy with a magnetic field of force, to denote the general domain within which currents of power and influence flow and interact. If the logic of that field is such that a number of different currents are all flowing in the same direction(s), then a major upheaval may result; and this, for Bourdieu, was the logic of May 1968.

Homo Academicus begins, however, in the present time, working back from a statement of its presuppositions and their theoretical foundation to an application of these to the May events. Bourdieu begins with a strenuous rejection of 'an "interested" reading attached to anecdotes and individual details',[31] in favour of a sociological knowledge which does not claim to be disinterested, but simply to take the scientifically necessary distance from its object of study. An 'interested' reading fails to distinguish between the 'constructed individual', an intersection of relations available only to scientific inquiry, and the 'empirical individual', whom anybody might meet walking down the street.[32] One might see it as a parallel, in the social sciences, to the conflation of 'the man[*sic*]' and 'the work' in literary criticism. Empirical inquiry, it is clear, is not a substitute for theoretical discourse, any more than the other way round; the two are indispensable complements.

The implied target of much of Bourdieu's criticism here appears to be Hamon and Rotman's *Les Intellocrates*, whose gleeful naming of names and profusion of personal details certainly privileges the 'empirical' over the 'constructed' individual. The work is not mentioned (to have done so would doubtless have been to fall into the very trap of anecdotalism and 'ad hoc explanation by ad hominem arguments'[33] that Bourdieu is denouncing), but its perspective undoubtedly coincides with that Bourdieu criticises in the interest of a proper scientific approach to the educational and intellectual field. What such an approach shows in the first place is that the university field, sustained though it is by an appearance of civilised consensus, is like any other a field of struggle, and particularly of struggle over labelling and classification. Bourdieu sees it as

> organised in accordance with two antagonistic hierarchical principles: the social hierarchy, dependent on the capital inherited and the economic and political capital currently held, is opposed to the specific, properly cultural hierarchy, dependent on the capital of scientific authority or intellectual celebrity.[34]

On the one hand, that is to say, the kind of academic (almost unchanged since he frequented Proust's salons) whose capital is social and political – probably a Catholic and a right-winger, with a large family and decoration for public service, and membership of one or more public boards or commissions, so that notwithstanding his lack of publications or more narrowly 'intellectual' standing he is incontestably one of 'the great and the good'. On the other, the left-of-centre Jewish *normalien*, with perhaps a plethora of publications to his/her credit but far fewer bourgeois symbolic and material assets than his/her opposite number. That s/he would in all probability not want these is beside Bourdieu's point, which is that social and class origin, institution of study, field of study, family structure and background, religious and political affiliation, and likely type of professional activity are all at work within the antagonistic logics of the academic 'field', in the selection of self-selecting individuals whose likely career paths are determined as much by an unconsciously interiorised combination of all these factors as by more deliberate acts of choice.

The examples Bourdieu gives of how disciplinary or institutional rivalry can affect ideological affiliation illustrate the (relatively) autonomous logic by which the academic field is governed, and how the repercussions of that can stretch into other fields. Thus, the dispute between Raymond Picard – a strictly literary professor-*agrégé* at the old Sorbonne – and the non-*agrégé* Roland Barthes, from the upstart Hautes Études, and thus tainted by social science and philosophy, is seen as the 'acting-out' of a multiply-determined rivalry in which 'roles seem to have been allocated in advance by the logic of the field'.[35]

Similarly, the roots of the 1968 crisis in the universities (Bourdieu makes no reference at all to its wider manifestations) can only be properly understood if the heterogeneities of the academic world are taken into account. The newer disciplines that had begun to make their mark in the 1960s – linguistics, psychology, sociology – often, as we have seen, recruited very differently from their more traditional forebears. Many thus came into the university system without the qualifications judged indispensable in other disciplines, and their recruitment severely restricted the career and promotion prospects of those recruited in more orthodox fashion. The almost organic rhythm of university generations, whereby the 'brilliant' student would prepare first the *agrégation*, then a *doctorat d'état*, and at the end of that trajectory be of an age to supervise doctoral students or judge *agrégatifs* – thus, to turn out youthful replicas of himself – was doubly broken, by the influx of lecturers in newer disciplines with non-'standard' qualifications and by those who came into more orthodox fields later in their career, only to find their path blocked (or so it seemed to them) by the 'young Turks' of psychoanalysis or film studies.

This is interesting as a detailed analysis of how the specific configuration of the French academic world caused it to reflect in its own specific way the sense of academic bottleneck that began to become widespread in the early 1970s. It is, for Bourdieu, as dangerous to homogenise the academic world into a unified whole as to deny that it is governed by a structural logic of its own. The determinants of the French university system (*including* its potential for change – Bourdieu is not a simple advocate of the 'ossification' hypothesis) in their turn determine the different currents that flow through its field. It is interesting to speculate how far Bourdieu, had he acquired the relevant statistics about the pre-

May academic world as soon as they became available, might have been able to predict the form the events would take.

La Distinction differs from Bourdieu's work on the educational system quantitatively rather than qualitatively, for it deploys much the same array of concepts – habitus, trajectory, aristocracy, and so forth – as the other works here considered. Where it differs is in its encyclopaedic scope, aiming as it does to take in the different ranges of taste and judgement across the whole of contemporary French society. The ambitiousness of Bourdieu's project is illustrated by the following passage:

> Thus, through the differentiated and differentiating types of conditioning associated with different conditions of existence, by way of the exclusions and inclusions, of the unions (marriages, liaisons, alliances, etc.) and divisions (incompatibilities, break-offs, struggles, etc.) that are at the base of the social structure and its structuring power, by way also of all the hierarchies and classifications inscribed in objects (notably cultural products), institutions (e.g., the education system), or simply in language, by way finally of all the judgements, verdicts, classifications, and callings to order which are imposed by the institutions specifically set up for that purpose, such as the family or the educational system, or which arise continuously out of the meetings and interactions of day-to-day life, the social order gradually inscribes itself in people's minds.[36]

The empirical work of documentation undertaken by Bourdieu is thus indispensable to his theoretical enterprise, and this is figured in the textual lay-out of *La Distinction*. Diagrams, statistical tables, accounts and results of surveys, interviews and personal testimonies at once interrupt the discursive flow of the 'main text' and form part of it, opposing a literal material resistance to attempts to isolate the 'theoretical' sections and bypass or ignore the mere edifice of fact on which they are based. Where Bourdieu more openly deconstructs Theory's implied claims to detachment is in his constant turning back upon themselves of intellectual analyses of or statements about popular culture, which conceal within themselves an implicit assertion of superiority. Thus, Adorno's critique of popular music is likened to intellectual writing about sport in that 'it makes it possible to express in impeccably populist terms an amateur's revulsion and nostalgia'.[37] The word 'amateur' here is evocative of the ideology of aristocratic detachment (of, precisely, *distinction*) that Bourdieu perceives not only underlying, but determining, the shifting fields of taste and judgement and the places that individuals, according to their various habitus, take up therein.

It would not be possible here to give anything like an adequate account of *La Distinction.* What is important is to understand how the work intervenes in the major French cultural and intellectual debates of its time. We have already noted the connection between the *nouveau roman*, that self-styled antipode of the nineteenth-century 'realist' novel, and the world of Theory. It is not fanciful to see in the dense array of detail Bourdieu presents – invoking almost every aspect of a 'constructed', individual's life-style, from musical and literary taste through choice of objects or scenes to photograph to taste in interior decoration and favourite type of restaurant – something of a latter-day *Comédie Humaine*, constructing in sociological form the kind of omnivorous survey of French attitudes and mores that was one of the things Balzac attempted in his fiction. That which, in the name of textual experiment (which is to say perhaps of an 'aristocratic' aesthetic of conciseness) was largely evicted from the domain of academically respectable fiction finds a place for itself in that of sociology, less 'distinguished' in its own right and thus less dismissive of the weight of empirical detail.

Such a distancing from the dominant intellectual orthodoxies of the time is most evident in the work's final chapter, 'Éléments pour une critique "vulgaire" des critiques "pures"' ['Elements of a "vulgar" critique of "pure" critiques']. By its very existence this is evidence for the deconstructionist view that texts are necessarily and infinitely multi-pliable, for it constitutes a critique of Derrida's critique (in *La Vérité en Peinture* [*Truth in Painting*]) of Kant's *Critique of Judgement.* Bourdieu's footnote observation that the widespread intellectual enthusiasm for Brechtian techniques of distanciation – championed notably by Barthes and Althusser – could be seen as a means of at once promoting popular art-forms and asserting one's distance from them[38] indicates the import-ance for him of the (class or institutional) position from which judge-ments of or about taste and aesthetics (including those which seek to deny both concepts in the name of a 'higher' political ideology) are delivered. It is this that he goes on to criticise in Derrida, whose 'philo-sophical "deconstruction" of philosophy is, once even the hope of a radi-cal reconstruction has vanished, the only philosophical response to the destruction of philosophy'.[39] Derrida, in other words, for all his irony, his privileging of the apparently marginal, his stress on the 'parergonal' (that which, like the frame of a painting, is at once inside and outside and neither of these), his conjuring away, through a multiplicity of rhetorical and semantic devices, of the sacrosanct Text, is still playing the game of philosophy, a game whose ground-rule is that the utterances it generates must of necessity mask their position in the 'field of philosophical production' and thus their position of privilege in the French intellectual world.

Bourdieu's critique seems at once apposite and unfair. Apposite, because the 'end of philosophy' which Derrida's work might appear (following Nietzsche) to mark, in fact provides philosophy with a new beginning, and because there are undoubtedly strong material and professional reasons (even if unconscious ones) why this should be so; as Bourdieu says: 'All those whose profession is philosophy have *a life-and-death interest, as philosophers,* in the existence of that deposit of hallowed texts the more or less complete mastery of which forms the bulk of their symbolic capital.'[40] Unfair, because it is easier to point to this absence in Derrida's work than to suggest concrete means by which the privileged position of philosophy might have been indicated in it; because Derrida himself, still a *maître-assistant* at the time this was written, belonged if any leading French intellectual did to the dominated fraction of the dominant (intellectual as well as social) class; because, finally, Bourdieu comes close to hinting that philosophers have no honest alternative to transforming themselves into sociologists, thereby escaping the otherwise inescapable aporia. Perhaps Bourdieu himself provided the best comment on his divergence with Derrida in his already-quoted remark in *Homo Academicus* on the Barthes/Picard quarrel; the roles seem, indeed, to have been allocated by the logic of the field. Bourdieu's criticism is much what one might expect from one occupying a dominant position in an academically dominated field, which does not so much detract from its validity as place it in the context it itself invokes.

It is the breadth of scope of *La Distinction,* and the stress it places on determinants of class and social origin, that cause it to rank among Bourdieu's most political work. Unlike many in the realm of Theory, he does not treat the 'relative autonomy' of the superstructural as if it were in practice absolute; the inheritance of class, family, and educational position, interiorised as the habitus and reinjected into the bearers' symbolic fields, is always there to forestall any such idealistic hypostatisation. It is not unfair to say that most intellectuals on the Left speak of the cultural worlds inhabited by those whose oppression they deplore with condescension (cf. Bourdieu on Adorno . . .) or not at all. The very 'workerism' favoured by so many on the Left (Maoist militants going off to evangelise in factories, PCF leaders denigrating the importance of any action not taken by the industrial working class, or simply Leftist lecturers and students sporting well-worn denim and smoking hand-rolled cigarettes) is but a mirror-image of the condescension it might appear to be opposing. Bourdieu's analysis, rigorously free from even implicit value-judgements, marks the French intellectual Left's first serious attempt to engage with the worlds of popular culture. It is its absence of condescension, as much as anything else, that places it firmly on the Left. None of the other thinkers dealt with here is difficult to place politically in quite the same way as Jean Baudrillard. Such a judgement would doubtless find confirmation in Baudrillard's own recent work, which has denied the very existence of 'the social', seen as a '"reality" already abolished in its simulation'.[41] For all his Leftist-sounding pedigree (contributor to *Les Temps Modernes*, translator of Brecht and Peter Weiss, professor of sociology at Nanterre), Baudrillard – denouncer of 'the unbelievable naïvety of . . . socialist thinking',[42] and author of the caustically demystifying *L'extase du socialisme* [*The ecstasy of socialism*] while the Mitterrand government was still in its 'honeymoon period' – effectively writes the political, as an area of meaningful activity, out of existence altogether. His answer to the question 'Where is politics?' would be: 'Everywhere, for those who are dupes of the political illusion; but, in reality, nowhere'.

What, then, is his place here? It can best be described as that of the Left's 'necessary outside': the marking of a limit as menacing (unlike the ersatz spirituality of the new philosophers) to the defenders of the status quo as to its opponents, revolutionary or not. Buadrillard's is not – at least overtly – the apoliticism of the conservative, holding that politics is of no interest to most people, who merely want to get on with living their own lives in their own way (a piquantly auto-deconstructive statement); it is that of the anarcho-nihilist, for whom the 'terrorism' of separatist or revolutionary groups is to be understood not through any self-proclaimed ideological justification of its own, but as a riposte to and denial of 'the terrorism of the social'.[43] This may seem to have points in common with the decentring, puntualising polymorphousness of a Lyotard or a Deleuze; but Baudrillard's pre-text can as profitably be sought in the situationist movement so active in May 1968. Serge Quadruppani, indeed, cites him as a major plagiariser of the situationist Guy Debord, in his commentary on a 1977 article in *Le Nouvel Observateur* by Claude Roy:

The overall champion of shameful copying and 'hushed-up' use, of 'burglary operations', is surely, in France, Guy Debord. Nothing is funnier than the care taken everywhere to use him without naming him, to tone and water him down (Baudrillard, for example [Quadruppani's note]) or when one can no longer pretend he does not exist, to rid oneself of him with a furtive acknowledgement (Régis Debray, for example [Quadruppani's note]).[44]

One undoubted difference between the situationists and Baudrillard, however, is that the former actively set out to disrupt, or even overthrow, the 'society of the spectacle', and to evolve in the process new forms of social relationships. Baudrillard, by contrast, is (quite literally in one sense since his early work is much concerned with the domestic forms and uses of technology) an armchair nihilist, who contents himself with a tranquil recording of the demise of the social (if it ever existed) and the inescapable entropy of Western societies. No doubt this is why Quadruppani accuses him of a dilution of situationism; Baudrillard himself, in the essay 'Sur le nihilisme' ['On nihilism'], suggests rather that he has recognised the inevitable next stage to situationism's purgative destructiveness, which is *melancholy:*

> It [melancholy] is not nihilism either, which aims in some way to normalise everything by destruction – the passion of *ressentiment*. No, melancholy is the fundamental tonality of functional systems, of the present systems of simulation, programming and information. Melancholy is the quality inherent in the mode of disappearance of meaning, in the mode of volatilisation of meaning in operational systems. And we are all melancholy. [45]

Baudrillard's early work, such as *Le système des objets* [*The system of objects*] (1968) and *La société de consommation* [*The consumer society*] (1970), follows in the footsteps of Barthes's *Mythologies,* and of such analysts of consumerism as J. K. Galbraith. It is possible, however, to detect beneath the demystifying thrust of Baudrillard's analysis the germ of his subsequent nihilism. The movement of consumer society at once towards standardisation and atomisation – that *locus classicus* of American liberalism and the new Left – is not, for him, an evil to be overcome by an effort of the collective ethical will, or a sowing of the seeds of revolutionary change at just the moment when material affluence might seem to have put that out of the question. Rather, it is the first step into the 'black hole' into which the individuals and groups that supposedly make up contemporary society are being sucked. The penultimate paragraph of *Le système des objets* is a straw in the wind:

> [the possession of consumer goods] can only outstrip itself, or reiterate itself continually to remain what it is: a reason for living. The

very project of living, broken up, frustrated, signified, is resumed and abolished in successive objects. To 'tone down' consumption or try to set up a system of needs that can normalise it smacks of a naïve or absurd moralism. [46]

Baudrillard, not unlike Lyotard in *Économie libidinale,* stresses the inescapability of exchange-value. Use-value, for him, is the imaginary product, not the ultimate referential determinant, of the various systems of exchange which function as 'ideologies', binding society together in a common misrecognition of their nature. As U. Santamaria puts it:

> Ideology is not be looked for at the level of discourses operating in the superstructure, but in the organisation of signs where it plays its role by concealing and dissimulating the social logic which is at work there. It lends credibility precisely to those illusions already exposed. [47]

In other words, to 'expose' the 'false' ideologies of consumerism, or the creation of 'superfluous needs' by advertising and the media, is merely to reinforce the illusion of commonality and freedom of exchange that acts as the cement of society. This is obviously an extreme position, for any communicative act at all, including Baudrillard's, necessarily fosters the same delusion, from which no escape seems possible, and while it is certainly true that ideology does not take only the form of 'discourses operating in the superstructure', as Bourdieu has shown, there is no doubt that that is one of its most important areas of operation. Baudrillard's privileging of the phatic or socially-bonding role of discourse comes close to denying it any communicative value at all. *A l'ombre des majorités silencieuses* [*In the shadow of the silent majorities*] gives an even more inescapably nihilistic (or even post-nihilistic . . .) perspective. The 'masses', for Baudrillard, are not the raw material of revolutionary social change, but 'inertia, the strength of inertia, the strength of the neutral', [48] and their power lies not in their potential for action, but in their passivity. They envelop and neutralise the appeals of 'State, History, Culture, Meaning', [49] and the proliferation of sociological discourse results, not from the growing complexity of the masses, but from their silent refusal of representation; it is an increasingly desperate multiplication of meanings that, corresponding to no pre-existent demand, have to produce their own.

Baudrillard's 'silent majorities' thus have – as the plural might suggest – very little in common with the sullen conservatism that the term usually connotes in Anglo–American usage. They resist, not only political or ideological labelling, but the very attempt to call them into being and endow them with any collective properties at all. 'No longer is meaning in short supply, it is produced everywhere, in ever-increasing quantities – it is demand which is weakening';[50] the exchange of information, opinion, and judgement on 'contemporary social reality' has no function other than the phatic one of conferring a group identity upon those caught up in its circuits. Information proliferates in virtue of a kind of 'Parkinson's Law', to fill and reproduce the social space allotted to it rather than to make referentially meaningful statements.

For the social actually no longer exists. That is to say, either it has never existed – it is an 'Emperor's New Clothes' of our time; or it exists absolutely everywhere, as the detritus of human interaction, a constant recycling of the waste of humanity; or it once existed, but does so no longer. Los Angeles – the city without a centre, the community that is not one – serves as an illustration of what Baudrillard's third hypothesis might mean. It is, by definition, impossible to 'prove' or 'disprove' any of these hypotheses; indeed, the major problem in dealing with Baudrillard is that it is impossible to deal with him, that the social and discursive nihilism he postulates is as unprovably irrefutable as the purest form of Berkeleyan idealism. In the last resort (if a last resort exists, which for Baudrillard is as unknowable as anything else), all one can do, following Dr Johnson, is to kick the stone of a political movement or an election result, saying the while: 'I refute it thus, sir.'

Not, as it turns out, even that; for the 'terrorist' movements that Baudrillard sees as the most significant ones of our time derive their significance, not through what they affirm (the bankruptcy of the bourgeois state, the oppression of this or that group, or whatever), but through their refusal. This refusal is (in every sense) a global one, which opposes 'to the *full* violence and to the *full* order a clearly superior model of extermination and virulence operating through emptiness'.[51] We are here much closer to the world evoked by Dostoevsky in *The Possessed* (a very influential text in France), than to the exegeses and justifications for 'terrorist' action habitually produced by the Left.

Electoral politics, unsurprisingly, get even shorter shrift from Baudrillard, the more so as his problematic implicitly denies the existence of social classes. *L'extase du socialisme* cruelly mocks the widespread intellectual enthusiasm for Mitterrand's victory, which for Baudrillard had no practical consequence whatever but was simply a poetic or Platonic dream, in whose presence ecstasy – that of the saints before the Beatific Vision rather than that evoked under the name of *jouissance* –

was the inevitable, because ineluctably passive, attitude. 'Socialism in power is merely another phase in the pretentious disenchantment of this society'[52] – this, because socialism itself is merely a simulacrum with no referent. Baudrillard's view is the inversion of the notion (attributed to Victor Hugo) that 'there is nothing so powerful as an idea whose time has come'. For him, the rejoicing in the academic and intellectual worlds after May 1981 was at once proof of how tenuous those worlds' grip on 'reality' (however defined) was, and a tacit admission that the 'social' is nothing but a simulation. Intellectuals could celebrate Mitterrand's victory much as they might have celebrated the victory of their favourite football team, and with as little practical consequence or commitment. *L'extase du socialisme* is sociology's revenge, not just on Theory or socialism, but on the social.

12 Conclusion: The 'Silence of the Left-Wing Intellectuals'

Baudrillard was not the only French intellectual to express scepticism about the Socialist electoral triumph. Émile Malet, in *Socrate et la rose*, goes so far as to assert that the intellectual world from the start manifested remarkably little enthusiasm for Mitterrand's victory:

> On the evening of 10 May, for the Bastille *fête* . . . the crowd of militants is a dense one, the firecrackers are joyous, the intellectuals are somewhere else. Before the presidential election, and during the months of the electoral campaign, the reticence of the intellectuals is remarkable . . . The Socialist Party 'apparatchiks' will wait in vain for intellectuals to be reconverted to socialism. The gap between the intrigues of the government and the reflections of the intelligentsia is so wide that it is becoming impossible to work together to manufacture 'ready-made' ideas for the masses.[1]

This view, for all its partisan exaggeration, does embody the major problems that have consistently dogged relations between the intellectuals and the Socialist government. It would undoubtedly have been naïve to expect these to be untroubled by controversy; the number of intellectuals who supported the PCF, in other ways considered themselves 'Marxist' as the new government did not, or made their main political investments in areas outside the traditional mainstream (as with Foucault and his work for prisoners' organisations), would alone have seen to that. That there was *a* government of the Left in France did not mean that it was *the* government of the Left that each and every intellectual would most have liked to see.

Even so, it is probably true to say that a majority of the French intelligentsia voted for Mitterrand, whether or not they found their way to the Bastille on the evening of 10 May. It would be cynical, but probably quite accurate, to say that one reason why so many of them did not was that they were carousing behind closed doors in the style, and the *arrondissements*, detailed by Hamon and Rotman. What Malet's prologue figures is the distance between the intelligentsia and, on the one hand, the 'socialist people' (to reprise a phrase of Mitterrand's) who did flock to the Bastille, on the other, the professional 'apparatchiks' in whose hands the reins of power now were. British readers will doubtless get a feeling of *déjà vu* at this point, for there are close parallels between the French situation and the coming to power of the first Wilson government in 1964. Then too, there was widespread rejoicing in the academic and intellectual worlds, but that was not long to survive those worlds' distance from the working-class Labour electorate on the one hand and those who exercised political power on the other.

'The intellectuals are somewhere else'; Malet's formulation echoes the 1983 debate in *Le Monde* on 'the silence of the left-wing intellectuals'. Those intellectuals who contributed to *Socrate et la rose* were hardly an exception, for most of them were former Communists (Emmanuel Leroy-Ladurie) or Maoists (André Glucksmann), and those who voted for Mitterrand had often done so on determinedly anti-Socialist bases (Bernard-Henri Lévy). The main theme that runs through *Socrate et la rose* is that of the outdatedness of socialism, suggested in a passage whose crassness cries out for quotation:

> Those in power in the PS, especially those responsible for the cultural diffusion of socialist ideas, show a disturbing cultural backwardness. In the age of Freud, Kafka, MacLuhan, Karl Popper, Michel Foucault, Pierre Bourdieu; when the streets are full of punk fashion, the 'hypercool' music of the Doors and Pink Floyd, the gastronomy of MacDonalds . . . here are our socialists churning out Rousseau, Jaurès . . . and the revolutionary epic of 1789.[2]

The confusion of dates (the Doors and Pink Floyd preceded punk by the best part of a decade), intellectual chronology (Malet seems unaware of the immense recent upsurge of interest in Rousseau), and ideological resonance (Karl Popper may be a fashionable 'anti-socialist', but Foucault and Bourdieu are something else again), is so comic as to make one suspect a deliberate strategy; but the implication is clear. Socialism (Touraine *dixit*, but also, more significantly perhaps, Margaret Thatcher and Jacques Chirac) is yesterday's ideology, than which there can be no more damning reproach. It appeared almost inevitable that the author of the contribution entitled 'La culture socialiste, c'est l'archaïsme' ['Socialist culture is archaism'] should be the ultimate neophiliac – Sollers, by now enthusiastically converted to his own brand of that newest of ideologies, Roman Catholicism . . . None of this is to deny that left-wing intellectuals early began to express doubts about the Mitterrand regime, or to resist its efforts to co-opt them publicly onto its side. Thus, Leroy-Ladurie says: 'very swiftly, the major intellectuals (Foucault, Bourdieu . . .) showed reservations that put them on their guard, in relation to Jack Lang [the Socialist Minister for Culture] or the Élysée'.[3]

It was, then, not surprising that the 'silence of the left-wing intellectuals' should have been so much discussed and debated. Philippe Boggio was to point out that the Socialist regime's generous offers of posts to its intellectual supporters had not been very enthusiastically received. Foucault was rumoured to have been offered the post of cultural attaché to the USA (though as we know, he was too busy with the second and third volumes of *Histoire de la sexualité* to accept); Boggio comments: 'The left-bank salons tried to make this contest [between the government's blandishments and Foucault's reluctance], which they followed with excitement, an index of intellectuals' independence. They won'.[4]

In other words, many if not most left-wing intellectuals – consistently with the non-*étatiste* view of politics we have seen so many of them adopt – actively resisted, even resented, the government's attempts to enlist them into its service. This ties in with the often-expressed notion that intellectuals are typically happier in opposition than sullying themselves with the exercise of power, and also with the fragmentation of the traditional intellectual's role commented on by Lyotard. *Engagement*, in its most obvious sense at least, would seem to have died with Sartre. Other themes that emerge from this series of articles and letters have already been touched upon, such as the intellectual world's blind spot for economics and the way in which the French 'star-system' encourages vigorous self-promotion of a kind not readily compatible with political involvement. The fascination with modern technology (especially in the USA and Japan), which united the Right, tends (according to Chesne in *Le Monde* of 2 August 1983) to divide the Left, between what might be called its ecological and its technocratic factions; and Henri Lefebvre makes the point (6 August 1983) that the 'American way of life' so reviled by the movements of May is now no longer a satisfactory adversary for the Left. What these observations point to is the ease with which the Right, in the domain of technological innovation as well as that of philosophy, could denounce the Left as old-fashioned – a recurrent theme in the discourse of the 'new' European Right, and one we have seen figuring prominently in *Socrate et la rose.* It was often enough pointed out in the *Le Monde* debate that the picture was not a uniformly gloomy one. Derrida, Guattari, Lyotard, the philosopher Jean-Pierre Faye, the novelists Michel Butor and Françoise Sagan, the composer Iannis Xenakis were all cited as examples of intellectuals whose support for the Socialist government had not wavered; and the most prominent 'defector' of all, the singer and actor Yves Montand, a former member of the PCF who in 1983 noisily embraced a kind of populism in which some detected the seeds of resurgent Poujadism, was hardly classifiable as an 'intellectual'. It was pointed out that many intellectuals had received support from the government to fund cherished projects (such as Derrida's Collège International de Philosophie), and that the conditions of intellectual and academic life had been improved by such measures as the re-imposition of price-controls on books. But the dominant note running through the correspondence, and figured in the very way in which it ground somewhat aimlessly to a halt at the end of the holiday month, is of the fissiparousness of the 'intellectual world', which at times appeared to exist only by an effort of hypostatisation. The death or disappearance of so many former *maîtres-à-penser* – Sartre, Lacan, Barthes, Althusser, shortly afterwards Foucault – in the early part of the 1980s reinforced on a biographical level a phenomenon whose institutional causes were multiple. The 'decentralising' tendencies of May; repeated disillusionment with the PCF; the perceived shortcomings of Theory; the new philosophers' exploitation of the media star-system: these have run like criss-crossing threads through our account, and between then go some way towards explaining the silence that so taxed Max Gallo and the readership of *Le Monde.*

There is another, less conjunctural factor that merits consideration, which has to do with the distribution of different types of power across the social formation. It is appropriate that it should be to Debray that we should turn, at the end of our study as near its beginning, for an exploration of this. He writes in *Le Scribe:*

Any institution of power prefers to be its own metaphysician. It is more economical and less dangerous to provide one's own metaphors. This is an area where delegation – the opposite of abdication – can swiftly turn into dissidence. So when a power is young it transcends itself through its own strength. In charge of its references, itself responsible for reproducing and distributing its governing values, it exerts a monopoly of legitimate unfluence. These periods so favourable for 'politicians' are unpropitious for intellectuals, who are immediately subjected to the organs of power and deprived of their scope for individual autonomy or corporate power. By contrast, periods of 'regency' or 'power-vacuum' (transitional regimes or floating periods) compel the central power to share its monopoly of influence, before perhaps having to sacrifice it and itself at the same time. These are, for the intelligentsia (lay or religious), periods of triumph and glory. Social cohesion depends on the intelligentsia, the privileged if not exclusive repository of all values, plans, utopias, and models of behaviour (in the Western world of the sixteenth, eighteenth or twentieth centuries).[5]

Debray's last parenthesis makes it plain that his time-scale is a much larger one than ours here, dealing in centuries rather than in decades; but the point he develops is none the less relevant to an understanding of the contemporary French intelligentsia. They were more prolific and self-confident in opposition, not merely because it is always easier (especially for an intellectual) to criticise than to administer, but also because they were the dominant source and repository of symbolic power on the Left. Once the Socialist government had come to power, a host of other discourses – now the voices of the State rather than of the mere opposition – were able to deprive the intelligentsia of their previous effective monopoly. If symbolic power is at once ideologically determined and necessarily finite, then a change of government will be bound to bring about a redistribution within its field; and the most obvious direction that has taken has been from the intellectual to the political. French left-wing intellectuals have on the whole been reluctant to follow that path because, as Debray says and the *Le Monde* debate constantly suggests, they have feared being 'subjected to the organs of power and deprived of their scope for individual autonomy or corporate power'. How the continuing dissatisfaction with the Socialist regime, and its increasing rightward movement towards social democracy, will affect the intellectuals' scope and their (corporate or autonomous) view of their political power is a question to which no answer can yet be written.

1 Notes and References

1 THE MAY 'EVENTS' – WHAT WERE THEY?

1. A. Gramsci, *The Modern Prince* (International Publishers, New York, 1975) p. 118.
2. R. Lourau, *Le lapsus des intellectuels* (Privat, Toulouse, 1981) p. 52.
3. J. Ardagh, *France in the 1980s* (Penguin, London, 1980) p. 531.
4. J.-L. Baudry *et al.*, 'La Révolution ici, maintenant', *Tel Quel*, no. 34 (Paris, 1968) pp. 3–4.
5. L. Althusser, *Lenin and Philosophy* (New Left Books, London, 1971) p. 163.
6. J.-M. Coudray, C. Lefort and E. Morin, *Mai 68* (La Brèche, Paris, 1968) p. 32.
7. A. Spire, 'Mai 68, mai 78 : dix ans, ça suffit pas', *La Nouvelle Critique*, no. 114 (Paris, 1978).
8. S. July, 'De la politique au journalisme : *Libération* et la génération de 68, *Esprit*, no. 586 (Paris, 1978) p.3.
9. R. Debray, 'A Modest Contribution to the Rites and Ceremonies of the Tenth Anniversary', *New Left Review*, no. 115 (London, 1979) p. 46.
10. Ibid., p. 47.

2 DISILLUSIONMENT AND THE ROLE OF THE INTELLECTUAL IN FRANCE

1. D. Kambouchner, 'La désorientation', *Autrement*, no. 12 (Paris, 1978) p. 82.
2. S. Quadruppani, *Catalogue du prêt-à-penser français depuis 1968* (Balland, Paris, 1983) p. 17.
3. D. Lindenberg, 'Adieux à l'intelligentsia', *Le Débat* (Paris, 1982).
4. R. Debray, *L'espérance au purgatoire* (Alain Moreau, Paris, 1980) p. 36.
5. R. Debray, *Le pouvoir intellectuel en France* (Ramsay, Paris, 1979) pp. 105–6.
6. Ibid., pp. 59–60.
7. H. Hamon and P. Rotman, *Les Intellocrates* (Ramsay, Paris, 1981) p. 233.
8. F. Bourricaud, *Le bricolage idéologique* (PUF, Paris, 1980) p. 66.
9. Ibid., p. 256.
10. R. Boudon, 'L'intellectuel et ses publics : les singularités françaises', *Français, qui êtes-vous?* (Le Documentation Française, Paris, 1981) p. 47.
11. R. Debray, *Le Scribe* (Grasset, Paris, 1980) p. 186.
12. Ibid., p. 140.

3　INTELLECTUALS AND MARXISM SINCE 1968 – SARTRE

1. J.-P. Sartre, *Situations X* (Gallimard, Paris, 1976) p. 97.
2. Ibid., p. 38.
3. P. Gavi, 'Bruay-en-Artois : seul un bourgeois aurait pu faire ça', *Les Temps Modernes*, no. 312/3 (Paris, 1972) p. 249.
4. Ibid., p. 195.
5. J.-P. Sartre, *Situations X*, p. 81.
6. Ibid., p. 86.

4　INTELLECTUALS AND MARXISM SINCE 1968 – THE STRUCTURALISTS

1. J.-P. Cotten, *La Pensée de Louis Althusser* (Privat, Toulouse, 1979) p. 56.
2. M. Kelly, *Modern French Marxism* (Blackwells, Oxford, 1983) p. 67.
3. R. Geerlandt, *Garaudy et Althusser; le débat sur l'humanisme dans le PCF et son enjeu* (PUF, Paris, 1978) p. 52.
4. J. Rancière, *La leçon d'Althusser* (Gallimard, Paris, 1974) p. 11.
5. Ibid., pp. 61–2.
6. L. Althusser, *22ème Congrès* (Maspero, Paris, 1977) p. 49.
7. L. Althusser, *Ce qui ne peut plus durer dans le Parti Communiste* (Maspero, Paris, 1978) p. 29.
8. Ibid., p. 92.
9. E. Morin, 'La mission des intellectuels', *Lire*, no. 74 (Paris, 1981).
10. L. Althusser, *Lenin and Philosophy*, p. 37.
11. A. Hirsh, *The French New Left* (South End Press, Boston, 1981) p.240.
12. E. Balibar, *Sur la dictature du prolétariat* (Maspero, Paris, 1976) p. 52.
13. Ibid., p. 52.
14. L. Althusser, *22ème Congrès*, p. 33.
15. E. Balibar and P. Macherey, 'On Literature as an Ideological Form', in R. Young (ed.), *Untying the Text* (Routledge & Kegan Paul, Boston/London/Henley, 1981) p. 94.
16. N. Poulantzas, *Pouvoir politique et classes sociales* (Maspero, Paris, 1968) p. 35.
17. Ibid., p. 44.
18. N. Poulantzas, *State, Power, and Socialism* (New Left Books, London, 1978) p. 16.
19. N. Poulantzas, *Classes in Contemporary Capitalism* (Verso, London, 1978) p. 199.
20. Ibid., p. 200.
21. Ibid., p. 256.
22. S. Hall and A. Hunt, 'Interview with Nicos Poulantzas', *Marxism Today* (London, July 1979) p. 198.
23. N. Poulantzas, *State, Power, and Socialism*, p. 265.

5 INTELLECTUALS AND MARXISM SINCE 1968 - MODES OF DISSIDENCE

1. H. Lefebvre, *L'idéologie structuraliste* (Points, Paris, 1975) p. 47.
2. Ibid., p. 118.
3. Ibid., p. 129.
4. Ibid., p. 192.
5. Ibid., p. 199.
6. L. Althusser, *Positions* (Éditions Sociales, Paris, 1976) p. 167.
7. H. Lefebvre, *La révolution urbaine* (Gallimard, Paris, 1970) p. 171.
8. *Modern French Marxism*, p. 180.
9. R. Garaudy, *L'Alternative* (Robert Laffont, Paris, 1972) p. 11.
10. Ibid., pp. 174-5.
11. Ibid., p. 195.
12. Ibid., p. 162.
13. S. Quadruppani, *Catalogue du prêt-à-penser français depuis 1968*, p. 68.

6 THE POLITICS OF PSYCHOANALYSIS

1. C. Clément, *Vies et légendes de Jacques Lacan* (Grasset, Paris, 1981) p. 45.
2. R. Lourau, *La lapsus des intellectuels*.
3. S. Turkle, *Psychoanalytic Politics* (Burnett Books/André Deutsch, London, 1979) p. 56.
4. J. Derrida, *L'écriture et la différence* (Seuil, Paris, 1967) p. 272.
5. S. Turkle, *Psychoanalytic Politics*, p. 122.
6. Ibid., pp. 122-7.
7. C. Clément, *Vies et légendes de Jacques Lacan*, pp. 175-6.

7 THE POLITICS OF FEMINISM

1. In S. Heath, 'Difference', *Screen*, vol. 19 no. 3 (London, 1978) p. 51.
2. Ibid., p. 53.
3. G. Hocquenghem, 'Subversion et décadence du mâle d'après-Mai', *Autrement*, no. 12 (Paris, 1978) p. 159.
4. S. de Beauvoir, *After 'The Second Sex'* (Pantheon Books, New York, 1984) p. 32.
5. J.-P. Sartre, *Situations X*, p. 120.
6. *After 'The Second Sex'*, pp. 88-9.
7. D. Maugendre, 'Lacaniens, encore un effort pour être psychanalistes', *Les Temps Modernes*, no. 381 (Paris, 1978) pp. 1720-1.
8. See above, pp. 19-20.
9. F. George, 'Lacan ou l'efet "yau de poêle"', *Les Temps Modernes*, no. 394 (Paris, 1979) p. 1793.
10. Ibid., *Les Temps Modernes*, no. 395 (Paris, 1979) p. 2039.

11. A. Fouque, in E. Marks and I. de Courtivron (eds), *New French Feminisms* (Harvester Press, Brighton, 1980) p. 118.
12. L. Irigaray, in *New French Feminisms*, p. 100.
13. L. Irigaray, *Ce sexe qui n'en est pas un* (Minuit, Paris, 1977) p. 213.
14. H. Cixous, in *New French Feminisms*, pp. 258–9.
15. B. Groult, in *New French Feminisms*, p. 69.
16. Ibid., p. 71.

8 LANGUAGE, POWER AND POLITICS – THE WORK OF FOUCAULT AND DELEUZE

1. R. Cobb, *A Second Identity* (Oxford University Press, 1969) p 91.
2. 'M. Foucault; Interview — I. *Pierre Rivieré*', *Edinburgh '77 Magazine* (Edinburgh, 1977) p. 32.
3. K. Tribe, 'History and the production of memories', *Screen*, vol. 18 no. 4 (London, 1977) p. 21.
4. C. Gordon (ed.), *Michel Foucault: Power/Knowledge: Selected Interviews and Other Writings, 1972–1977* (Harvester Press, Brighton, 1980) p. 10.
5. B. Smart, *Foucault, Marxism, and Critique* (Routledge & Kegan Paul, London/Boston/Melbourne/Henley, 1983) p. 122.
6. *Michel Foucault: Power/Knowledge*, p. 16.
7. Ibid.
8. M. Foucault, *The Archaeology of Knowledge* (Tavistock Press, London, 1977) p. 85.
9. M. Foucault, *La volonté de savoir* (Gallimard, Paris, 1976) p. 80.
10. M. Foucault, *L'usage des plaisirs* (Gallimard, Paris, 1984) p. 12.
11. This is a play on words, the French 'jeu' denoting both a 'game' and the 'play' or 'interplay' of the moving parts of a machine.
12. M. Foucault, *L'usage des plaisirs*, p. 12.
13. M. Foucault, *Le souci de soi* (Gallimard, Paris, 1984) p. 55.
14. D. Kambouchner, 'La désorientation', pp. 86–7.
15. G. Deleuze and F. Guattari, *L'anti-Oedipe* (Minuit, Paris, 1972) p. 362.
16. Ibid., p. 132.
17. Ibid., p. 434.

9 LANGUAGE, LITERATURE, DECONSTRUCTION AND POLITICS

1. J. Kristeva, *Semiotike – recherches pour une sémanalyse* (Seuil, Paris, 1968) pp. 34–5.
2. Ibid., pp. 204–5.
3. Ibid., p. 113.
4. J. Kristeva, 'La littérature dissidente comme réfutation du discours de gauche', *Tel Quel*, no. 76 (Paris, 1978) p. 41.
5. J. Ardagh, *France in the 1980s*, p. 531.
6. R. Barthes, *Roland Barthes par Roland Barthes* (Seuil, Paris, 1975) pp. 57–8.

7. A. Lavers, *Roland Barthes: structuralism and after* (Methuen, London, 1982) p. 205.
8. R. Barthes, *Le bruissement de la langue* (Seuil, Paris, 1984) pp. 121–2.
9. M. Ryan, *Marxism and Deconstruction* (John Hopkins, Baltimore, 1982) p. 35.
10. J. Derrida, *Positions* (Minuit, Paris, 1972) p. 100.
11. C. Norris, *Deconstruction: theory and practice* (Methuen, London/New York, 1982) p. 82.
12. J. Derrida, 'Où commence et comment finit un corps enseignant', in D. Grisoni (ed.), *Politiques de la philosophie* (Grasset, Paris, 1976) p. 64.
13. Ibid., p. 73.
14. J. Derrida, *Positions*, p. 17.
15. J. F. Lyotard, *Dérive à partir de Marx et Freud* (Union Générale d'Éditions, Paris, 1973) p. 9.
16. Ibid., p. 98.
17. J.-F. Lyotard, *Économie libidinale* (Minuit, Paris, 1974) p. 225.
18. Ibid., p. 118.
19. Ibid., p. 185.
20. Ibid., pp. 120–1.
21. J.-F. Lyotard, *The postmodern Condition* (Manchester University Press, 1984) p. 23.
22. Ibid., p. 29.
23. Ibid., p. 67.
24. J.-F. Lyotard, *Tombeau de l'intellectuel et autres papiers* (Galilée, Paris, 1984) p. 29.

10 THE 'NEW PHILOSOPHERS'

1. S. Quadruppani, *Catalogue du prêt-à-penser français depuis 1968*, p. 109.
2. F. Aubral and X. Delcourt, *Contre la nouvelle philosophie* (Gallimard, Paris, 1977) p. 183.
3. Quoted in ibid., p. 45.
4. P. Sollers, 'Le marxisme sodomisé par la psychanalyse, elle-même violée par on ne sait pas quoi', *Tel Quel*, no. 75 (Paris, 1978), p. 56.
5. Ibid., p. 58.
6. Ibid., p. 59.
7. B.-H. Lévy, *La barbarie à visage humain* (Grasset, Paris, 1977) p. 8.
8. B.-H. Lévy, *L'idéologie française* (Livre de Poche, Paris, 1981) pp. 83–8.
9. A. Glucksmann, *Les maîtres penseurs* (Grasset, Paris, 1977) p. 48.
10. R. Debray, *Le Scribe*, p. 61.
11. A. Glucksmann, *Les maîtres penseurs*, p. 326.
12. Ibid., p. 393.
13. V. P. Chilton, 'Glucksmannstalk: Packaging the Force', *Modern and Contemporary France*, no. 20 (December 1984), pp. 32–6.
14. Ibid., p. 35.

11   THE PLACE OF SOCIOLOGY

1. R. Rorty, 'Professionalized Philosophy and Transcendental Culture', *Georgia Review,* no. 30 (1976) p. 764.
2. P. Bourdieu, *Homo Academicus* (Minuit, Paris, 1984) pp. 166–7.
3. J. Culler, *On Deconstruction* (Routledge & Kegan Paul, London/Melbourne/ Henley, 1983) p. 153.
4. Quoted in A. Touraine, *L'après-socialisme* (Grasset, Paris, 1980) pp. 245–6.
5. Ibid., p. 113.
6. Ibid., p. 12.
7. Ibid., p. 49.
8. Ibid., p. 75.
9. Ibid., p. 215.
10. Quoted ibid., p. 272.
11. Ibid., p. 274.
12. A. Gorz, *Adieux au prolétariat* (Galilée, Paris, 1980) p. 64.
13. Ibid., p. 10.
14. Ibid., p. 143.
15. Ibid., p. 94.
16. Ibid., p. 95.
17. Ibid., p. 155.
18. Quoted in A. Touraine, *L'après-socialisme,* p. 258.
19. R. Nice, 'Bourdieu', *Screen Education,* no. 28 (London, 1978) p. 27.
20. See above, p. 100.
21. See above, p. 27.
22. A. Accardo, *Initiation à la sociologie de l'illusionisme social* (Le Mascaret, Bordeaux, 1983) p. 56.
23. 'Bourdieu', p. 27.
24. *Initiation à la sociologie de l'illusionisme social,* p. 15.
25. P. Bourdieu and J.-C. Passeron, *Les Héritiers* (Minuit, Paris, 1964) p. 115.
26. P. Bourdieu and J.-C. Passeron, *Reproduction in Education, Society, and Culture* (Sage, London/Beverley Hills, 1977) p. 5.
27. Ibid., pp. xi–xii.
28. Ibid., p. 11.
29. L. Althusser, *Lenin and Philosophy,* p. 147.
30. P. Bourdieu, *Homo Academicus,* p. 196.
31. Ibid., pp. 12–13.
32. Ibid., p. 13.
33. Ibid., p. 14.
34. Ibid., p. 70.
35. Ibid., p. 152.
36. P. Bourdieu, *La Distinction* (Minuit, Paris, 1979) pp. 548–9.
37. Ibid., p. 450.
38. Ibid., p. 568.
39. Ibid., p. 581.
40. Ibid., p. 581.
41. J. Baudrillard, *In the Shadow of the Silent Majorities* (Semiotext(e), New York, 1983) p. 86.

42. Ibid., p. 86.
43. Ibid., p. 50.
44. S. Quadruppani, *Catalogue du prêt-à-penser français depuis 1968*, p. 136.
45. J. Baudrillard, *Simulacres et simulation* (Galilée, Paris, 1981) p. 234.
46. J. Baudrillard, *Le système des objets* (Gallimard, Paris, 1968) pp. 262–3.
47. U. Santamaria, 'Jean Baudrillard: Critique of a Critique', *Critique of Anthropology*, vol. 4 nos 13–14 (London, 1979) p. 183.
48. J. Baudrillard, *In the Shadow of the Silent Majorities*, p. 2.
49. Ibid., p. 2.
50. Ibid., p. 27.
51. Ibid., p. 119.
52. J. Baudrillard, *A l'ombre des majorités silencieuses* (Denoël–Gontier, Paris, 1982) p. 108.

12 THE 'SILENCE OF THE LEFT-WING INTELLECTUALS'

1. E. Malet, *Socrate et la rose* (Éditions du Quotidien, Paris, 1983) pp. 18–19.
2. Ibid., p. 22.
3. E. Leroy-Ladurie, in *Socrate et la Rose*, pp. 265–6. (Jack Lang is the flamboyant Socialist Minister for Culture.)
4. *Le Monde*, 28 July 1983.
5. R. Debray, *Le Scribe*, p. 110.

Bibliography

Note: I would point out that the bibliography is *not* an exhaustive, or even partially comprehensive, survey of the field. That would have required a volume as extensive as the text of the present one. It is simply a list of the works extensively alluded to, or directly quoted, in the text, in the language and edition referred to in the footnote (generally the original French, but sometimes, for reasons of availability or convenience, an English translation).

My practice has been, with essays that form part of a larger volume, simply to refer to the general title when all the essays are by the same contributor (thus, Althusser's 'Ideology and Ideological State Apparatuses' is given page references from *Lenin and Philosophy*, the collection of which it forms part), but to indicate the author and title of an individual essay when it is included in an anthology (as with the Balibar and Macherey piece, 'On Literature as an Ideological Form', referred to as cited in the collection *Untying the text*).

Accardo, A., *Initiation à la sociologie de l'illusionisme social* (Bordeaux: Le Mascaret, 1983).

Althusser, L., *Pour Marx* (Paris: Maspero, 1965).

Althusser, L. and E. Balibar, *Lire le Capital* (Paris: Maspero, 1968).

Althusser, L., *Lenin and Philosophy* (London: New Left Books, 1971).

Althusser, L., *Réponse à John Lewis* (Paris: Maspero, 1973).

Althusser, L., *Positions* (Paris: Éditions Sociales, 1976).

Althusser, L., *22ème Congrès* (Paris: Maspero, 1977).

Althusser, L., *Ce qui ne peut plus durer dans le Parti Communiste* (Paris: Maspero, 1978).

Ardagh, J., *France in the 1980s* (London: Penguin, 1980).

Aubral, F. and X. Delcourt, *Contre la nouvelle philosophie* (Paris: Gallimard, 1977).

Balibar, E., *Sur la dictature du prolétariat* (Paris: Maspero, 1976).

Barthes, R., *Le degré zéro de l'écriture* (Paris: Seuil, 1953).

Barthes, R., *Mythologies* (Paris: Seuil, 1957).

Barthes, R., *S/Z* (Paris: Seuil, 1970).

Barthes, R., *Roland Barthes par Roland Barthes* (Paris: Seuil, 1975).

Barthes, R., *Sollers écrivain* (Paris: Seuil, 1979).

Barthes, R., *L'empire des signes* (Paris: Flammarion, 1980 [reprint of 1970 Skira edition]).

Barthes, R., *Le bruissement de la langue* (Paris: Seuil, 1984).

Baudelot, C., and R. Establet, *L'école capitaliste en France* (Paris: Maspero, 1971).

Baudrillard, J., *Le système des objets* (Paris: Gallimard, 1968).

Baudrillard, J., *La société de consommation* (Paris: Gallimard, 1970).

Baudrillard, J., *Simulacres et simulation* (Paris: Galilée, 1981).

Baudrillard, J., *A l'ombre des majorités silencieuses* (Paris: Denoël-Gontier, 1982).

Baudrillard, J., *In the shadow of the silent majorities* (New York: Semiotext(e), 1983).

Benton, T., *The rise and fall of structural Marxism* (London: Macmillan).

Bourdieu, P. and J.-C. Passeron, *Les héritiers* (Paris: Minuit, 1964).
Bourdieu, P. and J.-C. Passeron, *Reproduction in education, society, and culture* (London/ Beverley Hills: Sage, 1977).
Bourdieu, P., *La Distinction* (Paris: Minuit, 1979).
Bourdieu, P., *Homo Academicus* (Paris: Minuit, 1984).
Bourricaud, F., *Le bricolage idéologique* (Paris: PUF, 1980).
Clavel, M., *Ce que je crois* (Paris: Grasset, 1976).
Clément, C., *Vies et légendes de Jacques Lacan* (Paris: Grasset, 1981).
Cobb, R., *A Second Identity* (Oxford University Press, 1969).
Cotten, J.-P., *La pensée de Louis Althusser* (Toulouse: Privat, 1979).
Coudray, J.-M., C. Lefort and E. Morin, *Mai 68* (Paris: La Brèche, 1968).
Culler, J., *On Deconstruction* (London/Melbourne/Henley: Routledge & Kegan Paul, 1983).
de Beauvoir, S., *After 'The Second Sex'* (New York: Pantheon Books, 1984).
Debray, R., *Le pouvoir intellectuel en France* (Paris: Ramsay, 1979).
Debray, R., *L'éspérance au purgatoire* (Paris: Alain Moreau, 1980).
Debray, R., *Le Scribe* (Paris: Grasset, 1980).
Deleuze, G., and F. Guattari, *L'anti-Oedipe* (Paris: Minuit, 1972).
Derrida, J., *Positions* (Paris: Minuit, 1972).
Derrida, J., *Marges de la Philosophie* (Paris: Minuit, 1972).
Derrida, J., *Glas* (Paris: Galilée, 1974).
Derrida, J., *La vérité en peinture* (Paris: Flammarion, 1978).
La Documentation Française, *Français, qui êtes-vous?* (Paris: 1981).
Foucault, M., *Histoire de la folie* (Paris: Plon, 1961).
Foucault, M., *Les Mots et les Choses* (Paris: Gallimard, 1966).
Foucault, M. (presenter), *Moi, Pierre Rivière, ayant égorgé ma mère, ma soeur et mon frère . . .* (Paris: Gallimard/Julliard, 1973).
Foucault, M. *La volonté de savoir* (Paris: Gallimard, 1976).
Foucault, M., *The Archaeology of Knowledge* (London: Tavistock Press, 1977).
Foucault, M. (ed. C. Gordon), *Power/Knowledge: selected interviews and other writings, 1972-1977* (Brighton: Harvester Press, 1980).
Foucault, M., *L'usage des plaisirs* (Paris: Gallimard, 1984).
Foucault, M., *Le souci de soi* (Paris: Gallimards, 1984).
Garaudy, R., *Le grand tournant du socialisme* (Paris: Gallimard, 1969).
Garaudy, R., *L'alternative* (Paris: Robert Laffont, 1972).
Geerlandt, R., *Garaudy et Althusser: le débat sur l'humanisme dans le PCF et son enjeu* (Paris: PUF, 1978).
Glucksmann, A., *Les Maîtres Penseurs* (Paris: Grasset, 1977).
Gorz, A., *Adieux au prolétariat* (Paris: Galilée, 1980).
Gramsci, A., *The Modern Prince* (New York: International Publishers, 1975).
Grissoni, D. (ed.), *Politiques de la philosophie* (Paris: Grasset, 1976).
Hamon, H., and P. Rotman, *Les Intellocrates* (Paris: Ramsay, 1981).
Hirsh, A., *The French New Left* (Boston: South End Press, 1981).
Irigaray, L., *Speculum de l'autre femme* (Paris: Minuit, 1974).
Irigaray, L., *Ce sexe qui n'en est pas un* (Paris: Minuit, 1977).
Jambet, C., and G. Lardreau, *L'Ange* (Paris: Grasset, 1976).
Kelly, M., *Modern French Marxism* (Oxford: Blackwells, 1983).
Kristeva, J., *Semiotike - recherches pour une sémanalyse* (Paris: Seuil, 1968).

Kristeva, J., *Des Chinoises* (Paris: Seuil, 1974).

Lacan, J., *Écrits* (Paris: Seuil, 1966).

Lavers, A., *Roland Barthes – structuralism and after* (London: Methuen, 1982).

Lefebvre, H., *La révolution urbaine* (Paris: Gallimard, 1970).

Lefebvre, H., *L'idéologie structuraliste* (Paris: Points, 1975).

Lévi-Strauss, C., *Anthropologie structurale* (Paris: Plon, 1958).

Lévy, B.-H., *La barbarie à visage humain* (Paris: Grasset, 1977).

Lévy, B.-H., *L'idéologie française* (Paris: Livre de Poche, 1981).

Lourau, R., *Le lapsus des intellectuels* (Toulouse: Privat, 1981).

Lyotard, J.-F., *Dérive à partir de Marx et Freud* (Paris: Union Générale d'Éditions, 1973).

Lyotard, J.-F., *Économie Libidinale* (Paris: Minuit, 1974).

Lyotard, J.-F., *The Postmodern Condition* (Manchester University Press, 1984).

Lyotard, J.-F., *Tombeau de l'intellectuel et autres papiers* (Paris: Galilée, 1984).

Macherey, P., *Pour une théorie de la production littéraire* (Paris: Maspero, 1966).

Malet, E., *Socrate et la rose* (Paris: Éditions du Quotidien, 1983).

Marks, E., and I. de Courtivron (eds), *New French Feminisms* (Brighton: Harvester Press, 1980).

Norris, C., *Deconstruction – theory and practice* (London/New York: Methuen, 1982).

Poulantzas, N., *Pouvoir politique et classes sociales* (Paris: Maspero, 1968).

Poulantzas, N., *Classes in contemporary capitalism* (London: Verso, 1978).

Poulantzas, N., *State, power, and socialism* (London: New Left Books, 1978).

Quadruppani, S., *Catalogue du prêt-à-penser français depuis 1968* (Paris: Balland, 1983).

Rancière, J., *Le leçon d'Althusser* (Paris: Gallimard, 1974).

Ryan, M., *Marxism and deconstruction* (Baltimore: Johns Hopkins, 1982).

Sartre, J.-P., *Plaidoyer pour les intellectuels* (Paris: Gallimard, 1972).

Sartre, J.-P., *L'idiot de la famille* (Paris: Gallimard).

Sartre, J.-P., *Situations X* (Paris: Gallimard, 1976).

Thompson, E. P., *The Poverty of Theory* (London: Merlin, 1978).

Touraine, A., *Le mouvement de mai ou le communisme utopique* (Paris: Seuil, 1968).

Touraine, A., *L'après-socialisme* (Paris: Grasset, 1980).

Turkle, S., *Psychoanalytic politics* (London: Burnett Books/André Deutsch, 1979).

Vernier, F., *L'écriture et les textes* (Paris: Éditions sociales, 1974).

Young, R. (ed.), *Untying the Text* (Boston/London/Henley: Routledge & Kegan Paul, 1981).

Index

This includes the vast majority of names of people mentioned in the text, with the exception on the one hand of fictional characters, on the other of 'Marx' and 'Marxism', which unsurprisingly recur so often as virtually to figure as *passim* in the entire book. Movements or ideologies and those after whom they are named (e.g. 'Lenin' and 'Leninism') are conflated into a single entry. Certain political parties, publications, or other key events and institutions mentioned in the text are also selectively listed (thus, the PCF, *Tel Quel*, and the May events will be found here).